matters most!

CHOOSING
TO LIVE

A remarkable true story of adventure
and survival in the Amazon Jungle

DAVEY DU PLESSIS

ISBN 978-0-620-58239-1

First published and printed in October 2013.

Second print in December 2013.

South Africa

Cover design by Chanel Grantham
Cover photograph by Forrest Beaumont
Edited by Anthony Michael Posemann
Contributors: Robyn Wolff, Angela Voges, Bhanoo Sukha

www.daveyduplessis.com

To my father, Louis du Plessis, for passing on
an enquiring mind.

To my stepfather, Curt Wolff, for instilling within
me a deep connection with and appreciation for the
natural world.

To my grandmother, Naomi Spence, for inspiring
my journey of health and encouraging me to learn
more about the world.

&

To my mother, Robyn Wolff, for being my biggest
supporter and for always believing in me.

Thank you.

Contents

Foreword

As I was planning and researching for my first trip to Peru in 2012, I was lead to the website of a South African adventurer, who was attempting a solo source-to-sea navigation of the Amazon River. Intrigued to discover that he was also vegan, I became inspired by how committed he seemed to be to raising awareness about the current challenges facing our environment. I explored a bit further and through his Facebook page and YouTube videos, I was impressed to learn that on his Amazon adventure he had already summited Mt Mismi, cycled through the Andes and the Sacred Valley, and successfully negotiated some daunting rapids, on a tyre tube! Davey du Plessis was clearly a passionate and courageous young man, committed to taking action and willing to go to extremes for what he believed in.

While following his progress, I was shocked to read that Davey had been ambushed and shot while paddling the Amazon River. Relieved to discover that he had survived and was recovering in hospital in Lima, I felt compelled to send him an email, wishing him a speedy recovery and full healing. I was going to be in Lima a few weeks later, so I offered to bring over anything he needed from home.

I was pleasantly surprised by Davey's prompt and friendly response, saying that he did not need anything, as he would probably be discharged from hospital soon, but that I was welcome to visit him to share stories. When I knocked on the hospital room door, I was warmly greeted by Davey as we introduced ourselves for the first time. As he began to share his incredible survival story, I was immediately impressed by his humility, determination and passion for life. As he retold the details of the incident and explained how the selfless acts of kindness from the various jungle communities had resulted in him safely reaching hospital, I was consistently amazed at how so many elements had come together to ensure his survival. It seemed that if any one of the synchronistic scenarios had not worked out exactly as it had, it is unlikely that Davey would have made it. It was as if he was meant to survive; to literally 'live to tell the tale'.

Through his sharing of this remarkable story, Davey provides us with some fascinating insights into the workings of the body, mind and spirit, and offers thought provoking perspectives on the true nature of the human being. Davey highlights the importance that the mind plays in our perception of reality and how our beliefs affect our experience of life.

As you embark on the adventure laid out on the pages of this book, I invite you to proceed with an open heart and an inquisitive mind, to truly put yourself in Davey's shoes, and to consider what you would have done in the various challenging situations he faced. I encourage you to reflect on the experience in its entirety and, by observing your thoughts and actions, to contemplate how your beliefs determine your reality.

Davey du Plessis is someone who walks his talk and who is passionately committed to real change and trans-formation for the greatest good of humanity and nature. He enthusiastically encourages self-empowerment, doing his best to inspire individuals to take responsibility for their actions by considering their impact on the world. Davey is someone who is willing to stand up for his beliefs and to courageously challenge outdated thought-forms that are no longer serving humanity or the planet.

May the message that this story carries leave you with a renewed sense of what's possible; a reminder of the strength and infinite potential of the human spirit that resides in each of us. By embracing our weaknesses, doubts and fears and by committing to transform them, we give ourselves the opportunity to fulfil our unique potentials and to experience true freedom as we engage with life in all its beauty and magnificence.

May you find contentment and the courage to live an inspired and inspiring life, through sharing your passion and joy while living compassionately and constantly contributing through service to the greatest good for the greatest number. Above all, embrace every moment, remember to be grateful for all your experiences and live with a reverence for all creation.

Anthony Michael Posemann

Prologue

Challenges! We face them every day, some more considerable than others, but ultimately, challenges are one of the few commonalities that every human shares and faces as they journey through life. Often we are left feeling isolated by the belief that we are alone in our trials. Through this story I wish to provide a greater perspective on the obstacles of life and to reinforce the mindset that, no matter what the challenge, each of us has the ability to overcome and rise above what should be perceived as only an initial set back.

I realise that most of the advice shared in today's times very seldom translates into action, and noticeably, that those sharing the advice are often not using it themselves, a 'do what I say, not do what I do' kind of teaching. Through adventure, I seek to convey a congruency of thought, action and real life scenarios to highlight that any challenge can be overcome. In this experience I chose to focus on how a challenge should not poison the perceptions of life or humanity.

I wrote this book as an adventure story, but more importantly, as a subtle guide on adopting and understanding certain life principles – learning through story.

So, onward to Chapter 1 – enjoy the journey...

1

The Will to Survive

It is mid-morning, 56 days into my Amazon adventure and over a week and a half since I'd last had contact with civilisation. As I paddle steadily down the vast river, I notice a bird flailing around in the shallows near the opposite riverbank. I am too far away to distinguish what type of bird it is, or to properly assess what is causing its distress, so I decide to paddle directly across the river to investigate.

As I get closer, I recognize the bird to be a giant pearl-white egret, one of the more common bird species I had seen on the river thus far. The egrets I'd previously observed always seemed to be very shy, usually flying off before I was close enough to take a photograph, yet this one does not seem to be going anywhere. It is flapping its wide wings frantically, bobbing up and down, in and out of the water, rolling and pulling to break free. It is trapped and in a state of panic.

I notice that the encumbered bird has a hook embedded in its beak and see that the hook is attached to a small pole by fishing line. On this journey, I had observed how fishermen would leave hooks and poles in strategic places as a hopeful means of catching fish, but this time, they had hooked an innocent bird. The beautiful bird is visibly tired and noticeably stressed, and doesn't seem to have much life left in it. I realise that it has to be freed; otherwise it will probably collapse from exhaustion and drown helplessly in the murky waters of the Amazon River. I tie my kayak to a tree stump a few metres away, and wade tentatively through the waist deep water towards the anxious bird, with the intent of releasing it from its torment. I am so caught up in the desire to help this magnificent creature that I initially don't evaluate the situation properly.

As I proceed to within a few feet from the agitated bird, I stop. I grow cautiously sceptical as I begin to consider possible scenarios. Perhaps the fisherman is watching me, hidden from view by the surrounding jungle, and considers this bird a meal for his family. Maybe these traps are designed to catch both fish and birds, and it would look like I, the outsider to the jungle, am about to rob him of his prey.

I have my camera with me, intending to film the bird's release, so before I attempt anything further, I decide to act as though I am only taking photographs, to see if this draws any attention from the owner of the fishing device, who may or may not be watching me. I wait a few minutes; it seems to be just the hooked bird and me, all alone.

I take off my shirt to throw it over the bird to calm it down before attempting the release. Being so close to the impressive creature puts its size into perspective. It stands about waist high, with a wingspan of around a metre and a half. The blinding white of its feathers provides a striking contrast to the muddy waters in which it is flapping and struggling. As I am about to throw my shirt over the bird, it tilts its head and stares directly at me with one of its yellow ringed eyes. In that moment, I sense its helplessness and feel an even stronger urge to free it from its predicament.

I notice that its lower beak has snapped off as a result of its struggle to unhook from the fishing line. Its long slender neck also seems to be broken, but the muscles somehow still seem to be able to hold its head up.

As I move cautiously forward, the bird makes two big flaps with its powerful wings and I feel the push of air that this creates. The bird then becomes still, almost as though it realises that I am there to help, or perhaps exhaustion is taking its toll and the fatigued bird is just too drained to resist or put up a fight. With the bird now calmer, I work the hook carefully and gently out of its broken beak. Fortunately, I am able to remove the hook without a hitch.

I then proceed to gently guide the bird to the riverbank, where it stands firmly on solid ground. It is so depleted of energy that it doesn't even attempt to fly off. It stares at me for a brief second, perhaps in a look of appreciation, acknowledging my assistance, and then slowly staggers off, disappearing into the jungle. I realise that it may not live much longer, but I am pleased that I have done what I can to at least give it an outside chance of survival.

As I paddle off, my thoughts remain with the wounded, yet liberated, bird as I reflect on how it had probably been stuck for hours, suffering and panicking in its relentless attempts to get free. Despite being alone, with a broken neck and splintered beak, it was doing its best to stay above the water and, ultimately, to remain alive. I am amazed at its will to survive. What I do not, cannot, know is that in a matter of hours, its struggle for survival would become mine.

2

Unease

I hadn't slept much due to two powerful storms that came ripping through my campsite during the previous night. I had been paddling for a month, nearly two months into the entire adventure, but I hadn't yet experienced tropical storms of that power. That night it had been my turn to endure the might of the Amazon's storms. The tent, with me in it, was blown around like a tree sapling in the strong wind. All the humidity and transpiration from the surrounding jungle made for strong winds, powerful electrical displays and heavy downpours, all wrapped into sweeping storms, striking at will over the awaiting jungle canopy.

The second storm that hit me was so powerful that I had to pull my kayak next to my tent and grip it with one arm while holding the roof of my tent from the inside with the other arm, to prevent both the kayak and tent from blowing away. I used the kayak to anchor the tent and myself, while using the tent and myself to anchor the kayak. It was a wet, muddy and miserable night.

I eventually fell asleep in a sitting position and awoke early in the morning, still gripping the inside of the tent. Morning couldn't have come soon enough. However, the fact that I had managed to safely endure two storms in one night gave me more confidence in my equipment and in the limits of what I could withstand alone and in a foreign environment.

The morning remained overcast, with a slight drizzle caressing the dense jungle greenery. I continued with my usual routine, enjoying an oat and quinoa breakfast and packing up camp, to be paddling within an hour of waking. The sun eventually emerged, radiating its welcome warmth and gradually chasing the clouds and drizzle away. Despite the rough night, it was another pleasantly blissful morning paddling the Amazon's waters.

It was just over an hour after setting off from camp, and just as I was settling in to my paddling routine, that I was captivated by the desire to investigate and eventually unhook the struggling egret.

Soon after freeing the egret, I spotted a jabiru (the Amazon's version of a giant black and white stork) for the first time. As I continued paddling, a solitary pink river dolphin cruised in the wake of my kayak and later in the morning, a rare freshwater manatee popped up right next to me. It was the first time I had seen one of these odd looking creatures, which resembled a combination of a walrus, a seal and a small hippopotamus. It was definitely one of the stranger inhabitants of these mystical waterways that flow through the great Amazon Jungle.

I was having a good morning regarding wildlife interactions, and despite the miserable night's sleep, each encounter was a spectacular reminder of what a privilege it was to be in such a magnificent and largely undiscovered area with such abundant biodiversity. It was coming up to midday and I was in high spirits as I began to consider restocking my provisions.

A fisherman I'd spoken with on previous day had told me there was a small community, San Luis, a few hours motorboat ride downriver. I had estimated that I would reach the small community just after lunch, where I planned to resupply with drinking water, fresh fruit and vegetables. The river water I had been drinking (after boiling and allowing to cool) tended to have a slightly muddy taste to it, so I was craving fresh, clean water and was also desperate for something fresher and tastier to eat than the bland quinoa, rice and oats which had been my staple food source when fresh fruit was not available.

There hadn't been much human activity on the river that day and I hadn't seen any boats all morning. Just after midday, I spotted a small child playing on the sandy riverbank. As soon as he saw me, he ran away and stared inquisitively from a distance. I pulled up onto the bank and smiled as I shouted a friendly, "Hola" ("Hello"), trying to appear as non-threatening as possible. He seemed nervous and just stared at me timidly. I continued to coax him with questions.

"Donde est San Luis?" ("Where is San Luis?")

"Quanto oras es San Luis?" ("How many hours to San Luis?")

Despite my Spanish being very basic, the fact that I was speaking a language he recognized and to which he could relate, seemed to put him at ease, as he warmed up and edged carefully out of the jungle and towards me to provide answers. I understood that the community of San Luis was just around the prominent bend of the river up ahead, and he was confident that I could pick up some supplies from the small jungle community. I thanked him graciously as I re-entered the water, heading for San Luis with more assurance.

A few kilometres downriver, I spotted an oversized barge tied up on the opposite riverbank. I paddled towards it, hoping to confirm the boy's information and to acquire more detailed advice about where I could find the community. The river was a kilometre wide and when I saw the barge, I knew it would take a few slow minutes before I reached it. However, the wind had formed a chop on the wide river, which made the crossing even slower, and by the time I had reached just over halfway, the barge departed, heading upriver. I spotted a few locals standing on the riverbank, waving the barge off, so decided to head over to them to see if they could provide any information.

Even though I could not see any communities or infra-structure, I assumed that San Luis may be deeper into the jungle and that the presence of these people may indicate a place nearby where I could resupply and find accommodation.

I pulled up onto the bank and was met by a stocky, friendly-looking local. We got chatting, and he inform-ed me that there was a small town about an hour's motorboat ride along a hidden tributary that lay a bit further downriver. An hour's motorboat ride was equivalent to about four hours of paddling, so I decided that the effort outweighed the possible reward of find-ing supplies and that I would rather endure another week of paddling to reach Pucallpa than embark on an unwarranted detour. I thanked him and set off paddling again.

At about three o'clock a disturbing sensation came over me and I started to feel as though something ominous was about to happen. I fell into a state of deep fear and felt a sick worry come over me like a warm flush. I had, however, experienced this feeling to varying degrees several times since starting the adventure, and nothing untoward had materialised. Nevertheless, I hadn't felt this sensation as strongly or to such an elevated physical and mental state as I was experiencing in that moment. I resolved to push on with the hope that the feeling would gradually subside and disappear as it had on the previous occasions.

The sensation was diverted when I noticed a beautiful brown raptor sitting on the riverbank. Due to the low water levels, the riverbank rose up about seven metres from where I was paddling and the powerful, eroding waters had formed a muddy cliff. I thought it was very unusual for a bird of prey to be sitting on the ground when it had an abundance of towering trees in which to perch and survey the scenery. I whipped out my camera and began snapping photos of the stunning bird. It seemed to have decided to keep me company: it would find a small patch of clear land or an overhanging branch, stay there as I approached it, then take off and fly another few metres ahead of me, to land and wait for me again to snap some more photos. This continued for almost a kilometre. After a while, I felt like I'd taken enough photos of the elegant creature and decided to just appreciate its company and enjoy its obscure behaviour.

Although I became somewhat fixated on the bird, I still noticed a small-motorised peke-peke (pirogue) skimming the surface of the water about 100 metres or so just off the starboard side of the kayak, carrying two young locals, one wearing a yellow shirt and the other wearing a brown hooded rain jacket. I didn't take any further notice of them, neither did they seem to of me, and I returned to watching the mesmerising raptor as we successively progressed downriver.

The unnerving, sick feeling had passed, leaving me confident and excited about all the animal life I had encountered that day and looking forward with greater expectations to what I might experience in the months to come.

I was accustomed to estimating the time of day by the height of the sun and the heat. The humidity and heat had dropped and the sun was starting to touch the horizon of trees, which meant it was near the end of my paddling day. Day's end signalled time to start assessing the riverbanks for a suitable place to set up camp. What a great day it had been, by far the best day I had experienced on the river since beginning the adventure.

3

Ambush

As I surveyed my surrounds for an appropriate camping spot, I suddenly felt a forceful impact slam into my back. My arms shot up and my hands opened, catapulting the paddle into the air, like a double-handed shot-put throw. I let out a helpless gasped moan before I fell into the water, capsizing my kayak. My habit of closing my eyes as soon as I entered the water didn't hold, as I rolled, arms frozen outwards, into the water.

I looked around underwater and then towards the surface as I drifted further and further away from it in slow motion. I felt an unfamiliar separation between my mind and body, as I descended into this strange new world.

I couldn't hear or feel anything, and my senses seemed numb to the surroundings. In the green and murky underwater environment in which I unexpectedly found myself, the sun's illumination allowed just enough light for me to see my hands and the shape of my overturned kayak on the surface. I was sinking slowly, stunned stiff, as if I was floating motionless in space. The kayak soon disappeared from view and I shifted my blurred sight onto my locked and frozen arms.

I could not understand what was happening. I was trying to work out if the arms I was staring at were even mine. They felt separate from my body, as though someone had come from behind me and hacked them off. I was telling my brain to move them, but they wouldn't seem to listen. My arms seemed to be floating away from the rest of my rigid body.

The foreign underwater environment and the detached feeling were so unnatural that I could not piece together what was going on. I was trying to figure out how one moment I had been paddling on the river, looking at the jungle and enjoying the company of the obscure and friendly raptor, and the next, I had been plunged into the water, frozen in paralysis. Time slowed as I engaged in an internal conversation in which I tried to use thought processes to make sense of the confusing situation, and as I did so, the illuminated green turned to pitch black. Even though my eyes were open, I could not see anything but darkness as I continued to sink.

When I started feeling the sensation of the cold water on my skin as I sank slowly through it, I realised that my senses were gradually returning. My mouth was open and filled with water, and although I had not attempted to take a breath, I knew that if I didn't do something soon I would drown. This realisation initiated an instantaneous panic as I knew I had to get to the surface, or it was over. I wanted to use my arms to swim but they were immovable. It was a terrible feeling and I sensed myself slowly fading in complete helplessness. I began shaking my shoulders vigorously, trying to generate movement and resuscitate life back into my paralysed arms. I felt as if I was bound tightly in a straightjacket, trying anything to wriggle free. The more I wriggled and shook my body, the more I realised my arms were useless to me and that I was sinking even deeper.

The realisation that I was still sinking and that my arms wouldn't move forced me to start kicking vigorously in an attempt to tread water. I kicked as hard as I could, eventually emerging out of the darkness, rising into the green and back up towards the shape of my overturned kayak.

I burst through the surface and took a deep gasping breath to replenish the oxygen and provide some respite from the suffocated feeling I had been experiencing underwater. I felt somewhat relieved, free of the engorging depths and seemingly safe from drowning, but I remained in a heightened and panicked state.

I began to assess my immediate surroundings to determine what had caused the impact and the feeling of paralysis. I speculated that perhaps the raptor I'd been watching had flown into my back. I looked on the surface of the water for the bird and saw nothing but the overturned kayak. My vision was blurred from having had my eyes open underwater, so I blinked frantically to visually assess what was going on with more clarity. The blinking gradually cleared my vision, enabling me to view the riverbank and surrounding jungle, as I searched for clues as to what had caused this strange sensation and my current predicament.

I resolved to attempt a scream for help but stopped short of yelling the full word and only managed to say the 'H...' part of 'Help'. I was in such an elevated state of shock and was so fear-stricken that I could not make a proper sound. I tried to scream again but nothing came out. I felt so breathless that mustering up enough pressure to shout seemed like an impossible task and in that moment I realised that in any event, there was no-one around to hear my cries for help.

I continued treading water to keep myself afloat, as I sought out the cause of this foreign feeling. I looked everywhere, but all I could see was the river water, my overturned kayak and the riverbank rising to meet the thick jungle walls. The environment felt so alien that I could not even piece together why I was in the jungle. The only familiarity that I could relate to was my kayak, so I kicked towards it, my head bobbing just above the surface of the water.

My slight progress was suddenly interrupted by another severe impact on the side of my head. It was as if someone had taken a baseball bat and slammed my head, but strangely, there was no pain, just the heavy force and then a ringing in my ears. Bewildered, I took my eyes off the kayak and looked around frantically to try and see what had caused this sensation. I was expecting to see someone or something but still could not make out anything besides jungle and water, which lead me to suspect that perhaps something was attacking me from within the water.

The fear had elevated itself to beyond panic, and I didn't know how to react or what to do. 'Do I scream, or cry, or shout for help? Do I go back underwater?' The jumble of scenarios caused me to do nothing. As my head bobbed in and out of the water, I maintained my immediate priority as reaching the kayak so I could hold onto it to stay afloat. As I edged towards the kayak, I feared that I may be hit again by whatever it was that was attacking me, too scared to look anywhere beyond focusing on the capsized craft as some sort of refuge.

The strained treading and kicking towards the boat, coupled with my frozen arms, made the swimming process very slow. The kayak was only a few metres away, yet the distance felt like kilometres. Time seemed to be suspended. When I eventually reached the kayak, I hooked my left arm around its hull and managed to push my body closer to my arm, which allowed me to fasten the underneath of my upper arm and the side of my body securely to the kayak.

For the first time I could properly view my hands and arms out of the water, and I noticed that my biceps and forearms were tensed up, and that my fingers were bent crooked, clasped like frozen claws. I started kicking to propel the boat towards the riverbank. Luckily, due to my encounter and bump from a river dolphin a few days before, and the fact that I was following the raptor as it moved along, I'd been paddling only a few metres from the riverbank, so I didn't have much further to kick until I reached solid ground.

As I drew nearer to the bank I felt the muddy ground gradually swallowing my feet. I unhooked from the kayak and stumbled into the shallows. My arms were still frozen and locked in a bent position, as if I was flexing my biceps as hard as I could. By now my shoulders had relaxed, so my bent arms hung at my sides. When I let my frozen right arm hang down, I felt a sharp stinging pain in the ball of my right shoulder that indicated the severity of the impact.

I managed to wade through the water and mud until I reached a place where the water was about a foot deep. I then turned around and collapsed into a sitting position, confused, dumbfounded and scared sick. 'What was happening to me?' My body hunkered down in a crouched position and I felt what seemed to be holes in my back. Other body parts had no feeling, as if a doctor had jabbed me with anaesthetic, affecting specific and isolated areas of my body.

I had washed up into a small bay, which had been carved into a portion of the thick jungle by the eroding forces of the water. The bay protected me from the flowing water of the main river and allowed my kayak to just float in one position without being swept away, but it also shielded my direct views up and down river. The open and clear views of the jungle from kayaking on the wider and more open river had disappeared, and I slumped in the shallows feeling as though the thick jungle had hedged in my surroundings, restricting my sight. As I sat there trying to take stock of the situation, without warning, I felt another heavy blow to the right side of my head. It was the same feeling of being smacked in the head that I had experienced a few moments before, and again, I was left with a ringing in my ears. I'd previously experienced a concussion during a rugby game and I related this feeling after being hit to the feeling of regaining consciousness after a concussion. It was as if I was waking up in a new environment, not knowing what had happened only a few moments before, like an electric shock to the mind and senses that left me feeling temporarily numb.

My arms and upper torso were still frozen in paralysis as I rolled, baby-like, onto my stomach and looked at the jungle behind me to see what had caused this third impact. Again, I saw nothing significant in the thick jungle. I then rolled over and got back into a sitting position. My movements were uncoordinated and awkward. I was flailing around in the shallows, just like the egret I had encountered earlier that morning. I looked down into the shallow water and noticed its colour had changed – I was sitting in a patch of water stained red by my blood. I let my head hang loosely, staring in a daze at the bloodstained water, drooling and spitting more blood.

Even though I had not seen what had caused the impacts and the sensation I was feeling, it dawned on me that I had been shot. Someone in the jungle was shooting at me. I also realised that I was bleeding profusely from somewhere on my body. I felt so helpless that I didn't do anything. I just sat and stared at the blood for a few more moments, then raised my head to view the jungle walls across the river.

Seeing the pool of my own blood steadily expanding in the water, lead me to conclude that I was dying. 'Was this how it was all going to end?' Here I was, one minute enjoying the magnificence of natural life and the next, dying helplessly in a pool of my own blood. I could not even begin to contemplate solutions. I wanted to give up and disappear.

Everything seemed to be moving in slow motion and appeared to be suspended in space. The movement of the treetops from the wind and the flowing of the river seemed to stop, but were not completely still. The moments began to feel longer as the chatter in my mind quietened to focus on the sound of the flowing water. My mental patterns began to slow down, catalysed by the idea that time seemed to have lost its meaning. Reality seemed to be stationary. Confused, I lay back into the river with just my face bobbing out of the shallow, blood-filled water, resigning myself to the notion that I was dying.

I stared up at the intensely blue, cloudless sky. For a brief moment I felt selfish not to take into account what my death would mean for others. I was going to disappear in the jungle, and no one would ever know what had happened to me. Those who loved and cared about me would spend their lives hoping I'd somehow be found alive. I envisioned my mom spending the rest of her life hoping and praying that I would magically walk through the front door of her house one day. My untimely and mysterious death in the Amazon would leave her with many unanswered questions and perhaps give her a false sense of hope for many years to come, a hope that I was still alive, somewhere, hidden in the jungle.

Lying motionless, I waited for a sign that would confirm that I was dying. I kept my eyes open, as if preparing to see what death may look like in a physical form or perhaps out of a fear that closing my eyes meant the true end of my life. I fell into a trance-like state and became completely euphoric in the moment. All my fear and concern disappeared in an instant, and I felt quite at ease in accepting that I was about to die. I started to react to the warm and fuzzy feelings that engulfed me. I felt very comfortable and began wriggling my feet deeper into the soft mud, sifting the silt through my fingers, and revelling in the incredibly awesome high I was experiencing.

Perhaps it was the desire to feel something physical and tangible between my fingers and toes before I disappeared into the unknown, or perhaps it was an attempt to dig myself into the ground as a last resort of clinging onto my physical existence that lead me to connect with the mud. Whatever it was, I felt like a little child playing in the shallows of a muddy pool, happy and free. Fear and worry had completely left me. I decided to enjoy the process, assuming that I would be passing on in a few short moments. It was a beautiful sensation, as the sense of pure bliss seemed to increase the more I began to let go and accept that this was my end. My mind was clear and still and I no longer worried about being witness to my own death. I took a deep breath in and smiled contentedly as I closed my eyes.

4

An Introduction
to Adventure

It was through a serendipitous conversation at a casual Sunday breakfast that I was first introduced to the prospects of entering the world of adventure. Unbeknown to me then, but this interaction would also provide a gateway to an opportunity that began to reshape my ideals as an individual.

While eating a tasty fruit salad, I overheard Andrea, a friend, explaining how her brother, Ricki, was planning to cycle the continent of Africa, from Egypt back home to South Africa. This extraordinary idea immediately captured my attention. I drifted off into a silent dream state, vividly envisioning the sights and sounds of wild Africa.

"Is he doing it alone?" I inquisitively asked.

"There was an initial group of them, but they have all pulled out – I think it's just Ricki now."

My mind started working overtime, as it filled with inquisitive questions. 'So he wants to traverse the African continent? On just a bicycle? Sounds like the makings of an incredible experience!'

"Would he be open to me joining him?" I was unable to contain myself.

"I am sure he would, you should ask him," Andrea replied.

Despite not knowing Ricki, the idea of experiencing Africa from a bicycle seat had already captivated my imagination and spurred me on to further explore the possibility. I spontaneously sent Ricki a message, asking if he was looking for anyone to join him in his plan of cycling the African continent and if he would consider me accompanying him. He responded soon afterwards suggesting that we meet up, to discuss further. I took his response as a sign that he was open to the idea and felt a flash of excitement come over me as I started fantasizing more vividly about the great African bush and its wildlife.

I had previously been operating my own vegan food stall at a local market in Durban. The aim was to provide the public with healthier alternatives to fast foods. However, the growing business was dealt a blow when my car and all of my equipment were stolen. With those essentials gone, I couldn't afford to get the market stall up and running again and so instead resorted to selling and distributing the healthful foods from home. My focus was on promoting healthy and tasty alternatives that substituted the products of, what I considered to be, a pointlessly cruel animal food industry. I was doing what I could at the time to promote a sustainable and healthy lifestyle, which I believed, could only benefit the world. I yearned to be an agent of change, doing my part to contribute to a better life on earth for humanity and the natural world. Actively promoting a plant-based, vegan diet and lifestyle, which I had already adopted, seemed to be the best way of encouraging others to realise the sanctity of life in all its forms.

By the time Ricki confirmed that I could be part of the adventure, he had already done all of the planning and had finalised most of the details. The project had a title, 'Through Africa for Africa', and there was a credible organisation, Habitat for Humanity, involved, that would allow us to raise money while cycling. We were to take four months, cycling just over 9 000 km through Egypt, Sudan, Ethiopia, Kenya, Tanzania, Malawi, Mozambique, Swaziland and South Africa. We were to depart in February 2011, arriving home in early July. Ricki had organised for us to visit each regional branch of Habitat for Humanity along the way to give us credibility when asking for donations and to further help promote their good work in providing housing solutions to those who were most in need.

With all the logistics already taken care of, I began to focus on preparing myself for the cycling. I had no previous experience of cycling long distances, let alone cycling through vast countries. I had done some recreational cycling on the odd weekend, but had never attempted cycling any significant distances. Knowing that I would be expected to keep up with Ricki, who was an experienced long-distance cyclist, I felt it was my duty to seek an appropriate training schedule.

I managed to acquire a stationary mount, onto which I could fix my bike, allowing me to cycle in my bedroom. I was extremely enthusiastic about cycling through Africa and assumed that this enthusiasm for the adventure would motivate me to commit to this kind of training. The plan was to set up the bike on the mount and then, while cycling for a planned five hours a day, I would watch a variety of documentaries on the African wild, attempting to recreate what I envisioned the Africa cycle would be like.

However, after the first hour of stationary cycling I grew bored of just sitting on the bike, cycling and going nowhere! I was committed to cycling Africa for the sights and encounters and soon realised that I actually had no desire to adopt any cycle training regime. I decided that I would get cycling fit by cycling day in and day out, once we were actually on the road. It was the idea of viewing Africa from a bicycle seat and not the cycling itself that motivated me to attempt the adventure in the first place. I gave up the idea of training and instead chose to focus on my personal objectives for the adventure.

I had been a strict vegan for just under two years. I felt healthy and vibrant, but often encountered scepticism around whether this way of eating supported adequate long-term health. I decided that the Africa cycle would be the testing ground for my dietary choices. It wasn't that I had to prove the diet to anyone; I wanted to prove it to myself. The negative assumptions and opinions from others and from society in general were causing much personal doubt. If I could manage an average of 500 kilometres a week for four months in a multitude of environments, all on a plant-based diet, there would be no doubting that I was on my correctly chosen path.

The adventure would provide not only reinforcements for my chosen diet and lifestyle, but it would also be a way of testing my character. I had firm beliefs and ideals that pushed me to strive to have a positive impact on the world. I had spent several years working on my being, finding my internal pillars of strength and nurturing my strongest qualities of compassion, acceptance and understanding, but it was easy to have broader ideals and strong resolutions in a familiar environment to which I had adjusted and understood. Home was not providing the real-life experiences that could test my optimism, broaden my views or create a better understanding of life. I wanted an opportunity to test my character, to push myself out of my comfort zone and to stack the internal me against the external environment to see how I measured up.

With my mother being a psychologist, I was fortunate enough to have grown up with easy access to books on the mind, body and spirit. I found great solace in the inspirational leaders of my time as well as the various 'self-help gurus' who further helped me understand my position in relation to the world. It was these leaders, public speakers and authors who not only inspired me, but also provided some sense of direction. I too wanted to be able to inspire, to teach an understanding of life, and to embody a spirit of value. I felt that I had ideals, views and teachings that I wanted to share with the world.

Despite my accumulated knowledge on the mind, body and spirit, knowledge that I had adopted and incorporated into my lifestyle, I realised that I lacked the credibility necessary to make anyone want to listen to what I had to say. It seemed that each of my inspirational role models had their own stories - stories that provided credibility and congruency in their sharing of simple teachings and ideas. I also felt that I lacked the practical life experience that provided proof of the knowledge. No one was interested in a 22 year-old sharing views of equality among all living entities, or teachings on living an empowered and fulfilled life, without the life experience to back it up.

I had reached a congruency within but lacked the stories of real-life experience and the necessary action to support my views. I sought a story that could showcase the unlimited potential within the human spirit and I needed a story to inspire individuals to seek a greater personal fulfilment – adventure could be a way to find such a story! Adventure would provide the confidence to be able to stand up in front of an audience and share valuable theories on living and humanity. It wasn't my young age that meant I lacked credibility, but rather the life within the years I had lived. I knew that I had value to add to the world and adventure would be the springboard to get me to a place of credibility through action and experience tied in with knowledge.

Despite growing up in South Africa and considering myself an African, I had not experienced much of the continent. Ricki and I both shared the view that Africa seemed to carry a somewhat dangerous stigma that discouraged many people from visiting and experiencing everything it has to offer. Even though we would only be travelling through nine of the fifty-six African countries, we both wanted to use our experience to document, highlight and encourage more travel throughout Africa. We believed it was the unknown that created the 'daunting' legacy that embodied Africa as a whole.

As our departure date drew nearer, political and social tensions began to escalate in various African regions, including some of the countries through which we were going to be cycling. Egypt had just erupted in a mass overthrowing of its dictatorial government, remaining without a political system, as the citizens reacted in revolt. Sudan too had just voted on its secession, splitting the North and the South into two separate countries. Many of the North African countries seemed to have decided to resist and oppose their governments. Africa appeared to be in a state of political and social unrest.

Ricki and I found irony in the fact that a few weeks prior to our departure to Egypt, all tourists were being evacuated from the country. We were to fly in when everyone was flying out. However, despite the mass revolutions over much of North Africa, we remained committed to our decision to begin the adventure in Egypt and to keep to our scheduled departure date.

5

Through Africa for Africa

As Ricki and I departed for Egypt, we anticipated arriving in a country in upheaval and revolt. We knew that we needed to be extremely careful and that we would need to remain mindful of the situation at all times. However, once we were there, the hustle and bustle seemed to us to be how Egypt normally operated. It was only in visiting Tahrir Square that the unrest became noticeable, as we found ourselves in the midst of the mass protests and the occupation of the area. The chants from the large, intimidating crowds provided encouragement rather than fear and it was inspiring to be witnessing the action that would form part of Africa's developing path, as the people united to take back the power from corrupt governments.

However, despite our being aware of, and even at ease with, the situation, it was possibly a combination of our naivety about the general environment that we had stepped into, and our 'foreigner' status, that lead to us being mugged twice during the first two days of cycling. Unfortunately, we were victims of a blatant in-our-face 'we take what we want and there is nothing you can do about it' attitude. By day three we had been assigned a police escort that drove slowly behind us for the rest of our cycling through Egypt. The mugging experiences, more opportunistic than violent or malicious, very quickly offered the realisation that we had to be even more cautious and aware while cycling in any foreign country.

Despite the hostility, one of the highlights of Egypt was cycling next to the legendary and powerful pyramids in Giza. Reflecting on those remarkable feats of construction, I felt so privileged to be there and realised that perhaps the challenges we encountered only served to enhance the appreciation of all our experiences.

By the time we reached Sudan, I had settled into my rhythm. I was becoming a more efficient cyclist, easily capable of completing the minimum 100 kilometres of cycling per day. Sudan was an unassuming gem, which provided many spectacular landscapes, and I soon realised how beautiful a desert landscape could be. We cycled along the Nile River through most of Sudan, often seeing an unexpected abundance of giant trees and plant life growing alongside the river on our right, and desert and dunes for as far as the eye could see on our left.

There was a raw beauty in the presence of endless sand and emptiness, and it was at night that this beauty was most apparent. With no light pollution, camping in the vast deserts allowed us an intimate exposure to the night sky, as its detail was clearer than usual, with the stars seeming to shine more brightly. On most nights I chose to camp with just the mosquito netting shell on the tent so I could lie and stare awe-struck at the magnificent celestial display. After a long day's cycling, it was a real treat to be gently transported to a different type of dream world on the starry carpet of the Milky Way.

Once we reached Ethiopia, I was glad to finally be experiencing more of the essence of nature. The tree and plant life became more abundant, and we started to see more varieties of birds and insects. We had gone from the straight, long flats of the Egyptian and Sudanese deserts to the sky-scraping bends and turns of mountainous Ethiopia. The going was slow and tough however, worsened by the harassment of the locals, who would take any opportunity they could to throw stones and disrupt any of our attempts at settling into a pattern of just cycling. As each of the children screamed ahead to alert the next group that there was a foreigner in their territory, the surrounding environment would echo shouts of 'You! You! You!'

Despite its beautiful scenery, I didn't particularly enjoy the cycle in Ethiopia, which was further soured by an unpleasant altercation with a local.

As I was cycling, a man came running alongside me and nonchalantly stole my hat off my head and then ran off into the surrounding village. By that stage I felt that I had tolerated as much of the excessive bullying and harassment as I could, so instantly sprang off my bike and took off after him, eventually tackling him to the ground, and proceeding to wrestle with him to get my hat back. The small skirmish between local and foreigner sparked an interest in the community and before I knew it we were surrounded by several of the local men, who were now pulling us apart. I had managed to get my hat and ran back to my bike where I saw more of the villagers surrounding Ricki. The growing crowd was beginning to taunt us and grow in hostility. It was a scary few moments and we frantically put our feet to the pedals to escape the developing mob before things got out of hand.

I had never been in an altercation in my life, up until this mud wrestling effort to retrieve my hat. I was a bit shaken and was reminded that the vulnerability induced by adventure would result in a few new life experiences. It was another warning to remain constantly vigilant of everything going on around us.

The vegetation and natural beauty increased as we neared and entered the equatorial belt. Africa started to look and feel like the Africa I had imagined it to be, as the scenery included broad-trunked baobabs and varieties of birds and insects singing throughout the day among rolling mountains and hills of bushes and trees.

Reaching Kenya was a relief, mainly because I was glad to finally be leaving Ethiopia and the incessant harassment from the locals. The only aspect of the country I was going to miss was its food, especially the delicious Ethiopian avocado shakes and the variety of freely available plant-based foods.

We received news that a few weeks prior to our arrival at the Ethiopian/Kenyan border post, a group of cyclists had been shot at and had everything stolen from them. A few people at home who were following our trip initially assumed that it was Ricki and I who were the victims. Northern Kenya was stirring and becoming increasingly hostile, perhaps influenced by the mass uprisings spreading over many of the North African countries. Ricki decided that cycling that stretch had dangers that outweighed the positives, and he reluctantly, and in hindsight, wisely, decided that we would travel through the danger by car.

Due to the hostility of its northern parts, we didn't cycle much of Kenya, however we were still fortunate enough to get slots on two of their national TV talk shows. This was as a result of the entire cycling project being dedicated to Habitat for Humanity, which was doing a lot of work for the Internally Displaced Peoples of Kenya, who were the product of Kenyan political clashes and changing governments. The local media had taken an interest in what we were doing and were fascinated by our commitment to the cause.

Tanzania contained many of the highlights of the entire African experience: cycling under Mt. Kilimanjaro, seeing the ocean for the first time since we departed, and then cycling through a game reserve and getting up close and personal with an array of wild animals. Prior to cycling through the Tanzanian Mikumi National Park, my encounters with wild animals had been limited. Seeing zebras, giraffes and elephants from the bicycle seat was a totally new and sublimely awesome experience. These were the real-life encounters with the natural world that I had envisioned and for which I had hoped. It gave me a deep feeling of fulfilment and contentment.

Once we reached Malawi, we started to sense that we were getting closer to home, as the people and the environment started to feel more familiar. I spent my 23rd birthday camping under the brightly distinguishable stars of the African sky and fell asleep to the hooting of several owls as they called to each other through the blissful silence.

One of the more emotional experiences of the trip happened on an unusually tough cycling day in Malawi. Perhaps the long journey was taking its toll or perhaps I was just feeling more nostalgic as we neared the end of the adventure, but I spontaneously started thinking about the passing of my grandfather and began crying. It was probably the challenge of cycling up and down relentless hills mixed with long hours of pondering thoughts that eventually erupted in a flow of tears. I decided to pull over to catch my breath and in the quiet moment of the trees blowing in the wind, a small, beautiful butterfly landed on my leg. It just sat there, gently opening and closing its colourful wings, as I took a few pictures with my camera. It seemed so out of character for the insect, but that delicate butterfly seemed to be telling me that everything was okay. The encounter was encouraging and literally brightened up the rest of that day's cycling.

After three months of cycling I began to start longing for home. Reaching Mozambique aroused a sense of 'nearly there syndrome'. Despite the lush environment, I spotted very little wildlife besides the odd bird or road kill. Mozambique had been plagued by civil war and it seemed that the innocent animals had been affected too. I could not understand how humanity could have wiped out so much, all driven by greed and the pursuit of power.

After a few days' cycling through Swaziland, we eventually reached the border of South Africa – home! The familiar languages, car registration plates and advertising signboards of the 'in-your-face' messages from local cell phone giants further illustrated that we were in home territory. It felt like a lifetime had passed since setting off from Egypt, and finally reaching South Africa was a relief. I felt as if I had so much to share and the final few days' cycling consisted of warm smiles and waves from the many people who drove past us on the roads as we headed south in increasingly familiar surroundings.

Four months and nine countries later, Ricki and I arrived to a warm welcome in Ballito on the lush and beautiful north coast of Kwazulu-Natal. We were both relieved to be home, and after a few hugs and hand-shakes, Ricki and I went off with our respective families and friends. I had experienced and shared so much with Ricki and I struggled a little with the fact that I was going to be more than just a few kilometres away from him. We had been united in a mutual quest, living in each other's pockets for over four months, and the separation caused a slight bit of hesitation within me. I thanked Ricki for the incredible opportunity and highlighted what a privilege it had been to share this fantastic journey with him.

Witnessing the mass uprising in Egypt, camping in the isolated and ever-stretching deserts of Sudan, experiencing the ups and downs of both the Ethiopian people and terrain, cycling through a herd of elephants in Tanzania, swimming in the great Lake Malawi, being chased out of our tents by a raging forest fire and encountering the warmth of the people of home were just a few of the experiences that highlighted the incredible adventure that was Africa!

Despite the challenges, adventure had captivated me and I was hooked on the by-products and experiences that adventure promised. It was the platform that pro-vided a multitude of growth experiences and encounters that I was unlikely to find anywhere else. I realised that adventure provided numerous opportunities for me to be pushed out of my comfort zone and it provided the tests of character for which I longingly yearned. I had gained so much personally, and to add to the experience, I had been able to be part of a team, and support a worthy organisation, Habitat for Humanity, which supported many of the individuals we encountered along the way.

Adventure wasn't just a case of travelling through a multitude of different areas; it was both an internal and external journey that allowed much time for contemplation and reflection. Adventure provided the challenges for which I was searching, and took me closer to the deeper meaning for which I was seeking.

I had stuck to my strict plant-based diet throughout, feasting on the numerous fruit and vegetables grown in the rich African soil, returning home not only reaffirmed in my diet and character, but also optimistic about adventure as the platform that could provide the opportunities to put my knowledge and character to the test. It was an avenue that could provide credibility and life experience while further broadening my perspectives on the world and providing valuable insights into nature and humanity.

I had always had an adventurous spirit and a passion for the natural world, but I was now captivated by the idea of adventure and how adventure could play a part in the unfolding of my life. Adventure would be my story, a story that could potentially inspire and encourage other individuals who were yearning for the same fulfilment for which I had been searching. It was a commitment to continually push myself out of my comfort zone that aroused a deep desire to pursue further adventures and more experiences.

Despite my optimism and new-found realisations about what adventure could offer, as I started to plan the next one, I could never have envisioned just how far my adventurous spirit and my pursuit for an inspiring story would lead me, and to what degree I was to be pushed way beyond my comfort zone.

6

Run!

After several moments of waiting, and seeing only the black of my closed eyelids, I reopened my eyes and noticed that I was still lying in the same position in the bloodstained shallows of the river. I felt the water lapping at the parts of my face that were exposed and then lifted my head up to fully take in my surroundings. I looked around and noticed that my kayak was floating right next to me. Despite having been shot and witnessing the blood leaving my body, I realised that I was still alive. The reality of the situation was too overwhelming, so I lay back into the water and closed my eyes again, hoping that this time I would completely and blissfully disappear. I tried to shut my senses off from the physical world, attempting to feel what 'nothing' felt like, as if 'nothing' represented death. A few moments went by and I reopened my eyes. I was surprised to find that I was still alive and in the same place. Dying wasn't happening as I had hoped and expected.

Despite believing that my death was inevitable, I couldn't fathom what the process of death entailed. The euphoria was dissipating and my thinking was becoming more logical. I had heard and read accounts of near-death experiences and began to draw on these as examples of the dying process. Individuals had proclaimed encountering their gods, having out-of-body experiences, witnessing flashbacks or seeing a white light. Armed with these as some possible options of how to die, I closed my eyes and tried to force the vision of a white light or an ascending out of my body. I would think about what I presumed I should be seeing, then close my eyes and wait to see it. Despite my attempts to understand how to die, nothing further ensued. It was as though I was suspended halfway between life and death, but I didn't understand which one was beckoning me more strongly. I was attempting to think myself to death, as if dying consisted of measurable and calculable steps.

Yet again, I closed my eyes, waiting for something – anything – to take me out of the nightmarish conundrum, but again I opened my eyes and saw that death still hadn't arrived. I was waiting and hoping for death because at that point I could not perceive any other possible outcome. Death seemed like the most appropriate and only route; I just wanted the confirmation through some kind of sign.

After several more bouts of closing and opening my eyes, I was snapped out of this mental game by the sound of a boat motoring slowly upriver. I opened my eyes and shifted my gaze from the jungle walls in front of me to the direction from which the sound of the motorboat was coming. I immediately recognized the man in the boat as one of the men who had passed me only a few minutes before, while I was viewing the brown raptor. He was wearing a brown hooded rain jacket. I remembered that his companion was wearing a yellow shirt, and deduced that since he was no longer in the boat, he must have been the one that was shooting at me, stationed somewhere in the jungle.

I had been ambushed, hunted like an innocent and unsuspecting animal. The two men had planned to shoot me without warning as I paddled unassumingly down the river. They had obviously used the slight bend in the river to set up an ambush and had capitalized on the fact that I would not be able to see them until I was directly in the line of the shooter's sight.

The shooter's accomplice in the boat was about 50 metres adjacent to where I lay, heading slowly and directly upriver and towards me. He was obviously coming to assess the situation and to check if I was dead or alive. I must have initially appeared dead, as I lay motionless on my back in the shallows.

As soon as I spotted the man in the boat and then realised he was heading towards me, I felt a jolt of life surging through my body. I lifted my head completely out of the water and staggered to my feet. As I stood and rose up, the man in the boat noticed my apparent revival, slightly altering his course and direction from straight towards me, to rather heading upriver and monitoring me from a distance.

Realising these men's intentions, I attempted to plead with the man in the boat to leave me alone.

I begged, "Por favor, por favor!" ("Please, please!")

I clasped my hands together in a universal gesture of prayer, pleading for mercy. I was using any hand signal possible to try and rationalise with him. I made an effort to push my kayak away as if to say, 'Take it, it's yours.' I was so desperate that I did whatever I could in those few short moments to express that I was not doing anything wrong, pleading with the man to leave me alone.

The man just stared at me blankly as he continued slowly upriver. He looked at me as if I was nothing, staring straight through me as if I wasn't even there. It was a cold, cruel and sinister look due to the emptiness it portrayed. I was expecting some reaction but I received nothing but a haunting stare, bereft of any emotion. I had never seen such a lack of compassion or empathy in a human. It was as if he denied my existence. It was a look that only someone who had lost all emotion, or someone who had perhaps killed before, could successfully pull off. There was no anger or malice in his stare, just a void, as though his brain had shut off the synaptic connection between sight and response; seemingly awake, but hollow inside. I could not understand his lack of empathy or lack of response. 'How can there just be nothing?' I thought. He was acting as though I wasn't even worthy of a wince or smirk or frown. Nothing. I stopped pleading and just stared back at him, standing motionless in the shallows, watching him cruise calmly and nonchalantly past me as if I were just a rock and it were just another regular day for him on the Amazon River.

It was obvious that the man had absolutely no sense of concern for my wellbeing. He then took his gaze off me and looked ahead into the jungle and gave an ever so slight nod to where he was staring. I realised that he must have been looking to where the shooter was stationed, and that the nod was a message to convey that the job wasn't done.

I suddenly clicked and realised that I'd been trying to rationalise with the accomplice of someone who had shot me several times for absolutely no reason. It was the moment between the blank, emotionless stare and his gazing upriver to the shooter hidden somewhere in the jungle that sparked the inner voice, 'Run!' I had reasoned in that moment that if either of the two men reached me while I was still alive, they were going to do anything they had to, in order to end my life. Running was my only way of holding onto the very few moments of life I possibly had left.

I hesitated slightly before I took off, momentarily freezing at my kayak. I had left my Personal Locator Beacon (PLB) in the cockpit, and its potential importance suddenly gripped me. I wanted to set off a distress signal to notify the authorities of my GPS co-ordinates before I took off into the unknown jungle. As I turned towards the kayak, considering whether to attempt to turn it over and grab my PLB, in what seemed like a prolonged moment, another shot was fired. This time I heard it; sounding like two pieces of steel being clanked together, and I felt an immense impact in my left thigh. I didn't even attempt to look in the direction from where the shot had come, as this confirmed that, without any doubt, the priority of these men was to kill me.

I felt a surge of adrenalin pulse through my veins, any notion of activating the PLB instantly disappearing, and I instinctively took off running into the jungle. I could feel my left leg seizing from the shot. My breathing felt heavy and strained. My arms were still locked at my sides, which made balancing while running difficult. I assumed that it was the shock that was making my breathing so difficult. I felt as if I was extremely unfit, battling to take in full breaths. Despite this, I kept on running as fast as I could. The adrenalin called for me to run faster, to run through the pain and to get as far away from my attackers as possible.

As I ran aimlessly through the jungle, I suddenly noticed a large barge in the distance and decided to run towards it, hoping that perhaps I could catch it in time and be rescued. However, before I had made much progress I watched as the barge disappeared around the next river bend. After every few steps, I would twist to look back for the shooter and his accomplice, in case they were pursuing me as I ran wildly and awkwardly through the thick mud.

After what felt like a kilometre of sprinting at full speed, my body was screaming for rest. I stopped to gather my thoughts. I had been shot. I was injured and bleeding. The people who had instigated the attack and fired the shots were behind me, and the barge I'd seen had disappeared into the jungle, hidden by the river's bends. I was completely alone. I did not know where to go. The more I began to piece the situation together, the more overwhelmed I became. I could not even start to think of a solution. All I knew was that I could not go back upriver.

My assailants could both be back in their boat, coming to find me. I had been running along the river-bank, but thought that if they were coming to look for me, I was going to have to hide in the jungle further away from the river. However, I also realised that I could not venture too far from the river, as it was my only source of direction. The deeper I went into the jungle, the more difficult it would be to navigate and I could easily end up getting completely lost, thereby diminishing my chances of finding help. I decided to zigzag from deeper in the jungle to the riverbank and back, and to slow down, as this would ensure maintaining some direction and would enable me to stay hidden in case the attackers were looking for me. I had been running frantically with no direction to get away, but soon realised I had to formulate a clearer plan of navigating through the jungle as I searched for help.

I pushed on, heading downriver. There was a protruding bend in the river up ahead which would provide a lookout point to scout for possible help. The thick jungle hid everything, and I could only see what was on the waterways – the rest was a maze of dense vegetation.

I was still pumped full of adrenalin and despite my laboured breathing, seizing thigh muscle and locked arms, I managed to jog at quite a pace. I would look back sporadically to see if I was being followed. Fortunately, I never saw any sign of the attackers behind me. I cautiously emerged from the jungle and walked until I reached the open view of the bend on the river. From the water's edge, I had a clear view of about two kilometres up and down the river. I felt safely out of reach of the attackers, but was also out of ideas.

I collapsed into the thick mud, exhausted, hopeless, helpless and alone, trying to force myself to cry. I could not believe what had just happened. It felt surreal, dreamlike, and I wanted to wither away so that I didn't have to think my way out of this nightmare.

'Why, why, why?' I whimpered internally, 'Why is this happening?'

I had no idea what to do and the realisation of the desperation of my predicament was too overwhelming to contemplate. Despair started to set in. I wanted to disappear. I was going to rot and die in the jungle alone with no one knowing what had happened to me. My family would never know where I was or that I had been attacked and shot but had escaped. I felt so hopeless that I even reasoned that perhaps I should head back upriver to the community I had encountered before I was shot, even though the shooters might be locals there. 'Maybe they will show me some mercy this time? Maybe they won't?' I couldn't come up with any other solutions and felt trapped in a situation that lacked any possible positive outcomes. I had hit rock bottom. Wounded, and both mentally and physically drained, I lay alone and confused on the muddy banks of the Amazon River, ready to give up.

7

The Amazon Project

Ever since I watched my first wildlife documentary about South America, I had developed a deep fascination with the Amazon rainforest and the creatures endemic to the region. The documentaries I had seen portrayed the Amazon as a kaleidoscopic spectacle, with plants and animals that seemed almost alien. Even though I lived in a relatively nature dense Africa, the images that I saw of the jungle were certainly not what I was used to. The possibility of exploring the Amazon region's biodiversity and witnessing its variety of brightly coloured snakes, insects, monkeys, birds and other animal life strongly drew me to the region.

It was during the Africa cycle that I first conjured the plan to stage an adventure in the Amazon. At that time, I had no idea what such an adventure would involve or how the proposed journey would even be planned. I just knew deep down that I wanted to go there. I sought to gain first-hand experience and a greater perspective of this incredibly beautiful, yet threatened area of our planet. Once I had ascertained that I wanted to traverse the Amazon rainforest, I figured that travelling by water, on the mighty Amazon River, would be the best way of making progress through the dense vegetation and would also provide the best perspective of the jungle.

At every opportunity I had to access the Internet during the Africa cycle, I gathered as much information as possible about the Amazon region. How long was the river? What were the possible dangers and potential highlights? Had anyone done it before? What were the best ways of navigating? I had many hours on the bicycle seat to think about all the challenges and to devise possible solutions. The questioning and planning certainly helped to entertain my thoughts and occupy my mind during those long African cycling days.

I realised that in order to make such an idea worthwhile and also to give it credibility, I would need to take the adventure approach. If I wanted to represent a cause and learn about the area, I would need to traverse the more isolated parts of the river and jungle. Taking the tourist approach and travelling by boat to the designated attractive areas was not my idea of truly experiencing the region. Such an approach would also fall short in terms of providing opportunities for increasing my understanding of the natural world, and would not give me much credibility as an adventurer.

By the time Ricki and I had reached South Africa, I knew what my next adventure would be: a solo source-to-sea navigation of the Amazon River. The Amazon adventure would be an inspiring journey to a dream destination, aimed at promoting environmental action, while pushing me beyond my comfort zone and offering the potential of being a springboard to a career in public speaking and writing.

Within two weeks of arriving back home after the Africa cycle, I had decided to move to Cape Town and spend the next year focusing on the finer details of the proposed adventure. I still had much to comprehend and major logistics to organise. I already knew that the trip would need to happen in the dry season to make the navigation safer and more practical. This would give me a full year to do research and to plan the adventure thoroughly. I wanted to be in the Amazon by July, a year away.

Since I planned to attempt the navigation of the river solo and unaided, this meant that I would have to take all my own equipment and carry it throughout the journey. For the larger equipment I would have to have strategic drop–off and pick–up points where I could acquire the equipment required for each leg, while at the same time sending home any superfluous equipment which had already served its purpose.

The river contained a small, yet daunting portion of rapids and the initial plan was to hydro-speed down the white water section of the river, as another South African adventurer, Mike Horn, had successfully done. I would then paddle the open, flat water that made up the majority of the river. I had no previous white water experience, but had grown up surfing and confidently reckoned that I would be able to handle the rapids with some fins and a hydro-speed or white water body-board. The key objective was to start at the source of the Amazon River and to use as much of the river as possible to reach my ultimate goal: the river's meeting with the sea on Brazil's Atlantic coastline.

The river and its tributaries spread widely across much of central South America, but the documented true source of the Amazon was in Peru. Traversing the entire river would see me navigating through a section of the Peruvian Andes, heading north towards Colombia, where the river takes an almost 90° bend east into Brazil, and then cutting across the South American continent until the river's meeting with the Atlantic Ocean – a 6 500 kilometre stretch of river, flowing through the world's largest rainforest. I projected that I could complete the navigation in just over four months, with a maximum of five. I surmised that as long as I covered at least 50 kilometres per day, I would easily reach the Brazilian coastline in the estimated time frame.

Having reliable equipment and well-organised logistics are crucial aspects of a successful adventure. I knew that my daily living costs on the adventure would be minimal, but that the equipment, flights, insurance and other logistics would require significant funding. I began my search for a sponsor by sending emails to corporations that I thought might be interested in supporting what I saw as an incredibly worthwhile project. The idea was that the sponsor would provide funds and equipment in exchange for media representation and authentic brand recognition throughout the journey, and more importantly, that the sponsor would be affiliated with an individual embarking on an epic adventure for a worthy cause. I saw it as a wonderful and substantial opportunity for any business, and I expected that many a company would want to be linked to such an awesome adventure.

However, my numerous emails and follow-up calls to potential sponsors were consistently met with no interest, leading me to realise just how naive my assumptions had been. I did have a previous connection with a clothing sponsor from my cycle through Africa and fortunately managed to re-sign a contract with them that provided the vital clothing I required for this next adventure. I also managed to gain a few small product sponsorships here and there: a pair of shoes and mosquito spray. While I was grateful for these contributions, I had yet to secure sponsorship of a scale that would fund the adventure. Time seemed to be running out. With a few months to go to my proposed departure date, I still had no financial sponsorship, which meant that the adventure was still just a plan. Until I could buy the flight tickets, the adventure would remain nothing but a pipe dream.

After having represented Habitat for Humanity during the Africa cycle, I knew that I wanted the Amazon project to represent a similarly worthy organisation. However, after seeing first-hand the ineffectiveness of many of the other humanitarian organisations spread across Africa, I had become somewhat sceptical of the Aid sector in general. I was only willing to represent an organisation that was dedicated to long-term solutions and meaningful empowerment, not an organisation whose involvement was limited to pretty signs and PowerPoint presentations aimed at enticing and satisfying donors. The number of organisations in Africa, and their apparent ineptitude, concerned me.

Given the nature of the Amazon adventure and the environmental cause it would represent, the World Wildlife Fund (WWF) seemed to be the most appropriate and credible organisation to affiliate with the project. I believed that since the WWF was a worldwide organisation, it was in a position to promote conservation extremely effectively on a global basis, and I was willing to spread its messages wherever I was on the planet. The WWF initially seemed interested in the project, yet remained doubtful of their involvement for a few reasons. Firstly, I would only be a temporary ambassador for the organisation, and they sought a longer-term association. While I wasn't against this concept, it wasn't something I was willing to commit to at that point. Secondly, there was a conflict of interest: I was a South African staging an adventure in South America, which resulted in a regional conflict between WWF Brazil and WWF South Africa. WWF representation for the adventure would require clearance and acceptance from WWF Brazil. Despite much correspondence, I was never given final confirmation to represent the WWF, and accepted that it was not meant to be.

Undeterred by this apparent let down, I remained committed to representing a great cause. Without one, I felt that the adventure had no purpose or meaning. There were options to support programmes in which one could buy trees in the Amazon, but after much following up, I decided against representing these initiatives because the organisations would not allow me to visit the areas of the trees that I could raise funds to buy. I was not willing to accept donations from supporters under these circumstances.

Not succeeding in finding an organisation to represent eventually turned out to be a blessing. It alleviated the additional responsibility of me being expected to collect and raise funds throughout the project. I had also never particularly liked the idea of asking people to donate their money to something with intangible results. 'What am I really donating to?' This question continued to linger since my witnessing many organisations' seemingly ineffective work in Africa.

I wanted the Amazon adventure to promote sustainable actions that every individual could take in order to minimize his or her impact on the earth. The aim was to encourage 'donated actions' as the only form of currency required during the adventure. I was not focused on any clear-cut solutions, rather, I wanted to highlight individual responsibility towards global issues, and to encourage a move away from a dependence on governments, corporations and organisations to produce effective change.

I wished to address the source of the many environmental issues facing our planet, the source being humanity's modern lifestyle. I felt that encouraging and promoting individual responsibility was the best way to inspire change. Donating money only seemed to perpetuate a continuous cycle of merely treating the symptoms. I was dedicated to real change, the vital change that was so desperately needed, and I had made sure that I had adopted every aspect of a life that I promoted. I could never understand how some individuals were promoting causes and ideals that they hadn't actually adopted as part of their own lifestyles.

I was also starting to see how representing a cause could become an ego-driven desire to appear glamorous in the eyes of the supporters. Adventure provided a privileged public platform and I wanted to make sure that I was authentically promoting a cause that I believed in, and towards which I had dedicated my life. I had reached that congruency within, acknowledging the benefits of my choices and I wanted to allow the adventure to be the broader platform to promote actions based on research, observations, ideals and knowledge.

So it was that I finalised my adventure's concept and cause as 'Empowerment for the Environment'. I posted the cause on my website, planning to use the initial concept of an adventure in the Amazon to be the magnet that could further publicise the cause. The cause was the focus and I wanted to reach out to a greater audience than just those individuals interested in the adventure aspect of the project.

Despite not finding a suitable organisation to represent, I managed to team up with Adventurers and Scientists for Conservation (ASC), an organisation that designates areas from which adventurers collect research data about the environment and endemic species. The information from an adventurer is then relayed to an assigned scientist, who compiles the data to highlight problem areas and promote certain environmental initiatives. This was a wonderfully symbiotic collaboration, which ultimately gave the adventure a greater purpose.

With just under two months to go to my projected departure, I began to grow more sceptical about the idea of hydro-speeding on the white water leg. During my planning, I had been in contact with Tim Biggs, the only person to have paddled all three of the Amazon River's main tributaries. Fortunately, he had also moved to Cape Town, which allowed weekly visits to learn about the rivers and to gain some insights into my hydro-speeding dilemma. Tim warned that the white water I planned to hydro-speed was some of the most dangerous he had ever experienced, and elaborated that most of the rapids channelled through steep valley walls which made portaging nearly impossible.

He emphasized, "Once you are in it, you are in it!"

The idea of being trapped in a deep canyon with heavy white water and no portage opportunity confirmed my scepticism and put a huge dampener on my initial prospects of hydro-speeding. Only an estimated 800 kilometres of the proposed 6 500 kilometre journey included heavy white water, but those 800 kilometres could make or break the entire adventure, and me. I acknowledged that I was inexperienced and that I was not prepared to put my life in the hands of the white water, so I needed to devise a new plan to overcome this challenge.

On my third visit with Tim, we were poring over maps and discussing how I could navigate the rapids, when Tim had a light-bulb moment, and exclaimed, "You have just cycled through Africa, right?"

It suddenly clicked.

"Why not cycle, following the tributary?" Tim suggested, as he pointed to the roads that ran adjacent to much of the white water sections of the river.

It was the obvious solution, and so it was settled: cycling, rather than hydro-speeding, would ensure my safe passage for the second stage of the journey. I could possibly even cover the stage in less time than if I was to hydro-speed, and I would be remaining true to using only human-powered transportation, one of the essential criteria I had set for the adventure. I was relieved to have found a solution and became jubilant at the new prospect of cycling through the Peruvian Andes. I felt a surge of joy and confidence flood through me. After all the speculation and logistical challenges of finding a solution to navigating the rapids section of the river, I finally knew how I would do it. My itinerary and plan could now be properly organised and finalised.

I decided to divide the adventure into three stages. The first stage would be a hike to the summit of Mount Mismi, noted as the true source, where the first drops of glacial melt water eventually form the mighty Amazon River. The second stage would involve cycling an estimated 800 kilometres alongside one of the Amazon River's main tributaries, through the Peruvian Andes. I would finally reach flat water and begin the third and final stage: a 5 700 kilometre kayak paddle of the Amazon River to the Atlantic Ocean on the coast of Brazil (see Amazon Project map on page 101).

I would fly out of South Africa with my bicycle, complete the hike and bike ride, and then return to Lima, from where I would send my bicycle home and collect the kayak, which I would have posted to me in the meantime. I would then return to the river to start paddling.

Everything seemed to be coming together, slowly but surely. I remained confident in the project, despite having yet to secure financial backing.

Although the website was already in the public domain, I chose not to publicise the adventure any further until I was certain that I had the finances to turn the idea into a reality. I would only consider the project to be legitimate once I had flights booked to Peru. I remained deeply passionate about the project, despite the pessimism, lack of support and disinterest from many potential sponsors. Naturally, I discussed the project almost daily with my family, discussions which, I assume, eventually resulted in my mother's partner, MJ, offering to sponsor the adventure. I suspect my passion and enthusiasm resulted in him wanting to be a part of such a purposeful project. He shared my vision.

So after just over a year of planning, everything had come together in the final three months. The fundamentals of what made the adventure possible and worthwhile were all in place: I had a cause, a route and a way of financing the project to turn the dream into a reality.

However, the most daunting part of having everything sorted out was that I then had nothing else to focus on besides the perceived experiences of the adventure! I started to have sleepless nights, imagining what it would be like to camp alone in the middle of the Amazon Jungle. The density of the vegetation, and the perceived sounds, began to put me into an anxious headspace. Now that it was actually happening, I doubted whether I had what it would demand from me to endure the jungle, solitude and foreign environment. Despite these niggling doubts, I was committed. A few weeks prior to my departure I signed up for a few Spanish and Portuguese classes in the hope of picking up the basics of each language before I left. I speculated that this would be valuable in communicating with the locals along the route.

Shortly after my 24th birthday, I said a few goodbyes to friends and had a warm send-off from Cape Town International Airport by my mother, brother (Richie) and girlfriend (Chanel). None of us had any real idea of what to expect or what would happen in the next few months. I had planned as much as I could and departed from South Africa bound for Peru feeling suitably prepared for whatever it was that I was about to experience in the jungles of the Amazon.

8

Locating the Source

I arrived in Lima feeling somewhat daunted by the upcoming enormity of what I was attempting, yet at the same time I felt well prepared and undeniably excited for what I anticipated would be a spectacular adventure. I made my way from Lima to Tuti, arriving there with two days to spare before my planned departure to locate the source of the Amazon River, a 5 700 metre glacier-capped mountain peak known as Mount Mismi. According to the most up to date data at the time, the melt water off the peak was the true source of the Amazon River, and so reaching the summit would be the official start of the adventure.

Through my research, I had found that Tuti was the closest town to the Mount Mismi peak, and had decided to use the town as my base for the first leg of the adventure. I would leave my bicycle, and the other equipment that I did not require for my attempted ascent, in the town.

Tuti lay hidden in the vast and magnificent Colca Canyon. The community had relatively little to offer in terms of amenities and tourism. It was the middle of winter and the extreme cold was emphasized by the deserted streets, with more lone donkeys, dogs and goats to greet than people.

The remote town had two restaurants, each really just a section of someone's living room adapted to accommodate hungry foreign visitors. The shops were all similar as they sold mostly the same commercial products. Most of the small businesses and households remained closed for the majority of the day, perhaps due to the winter chill or lack of customers, or a combination of both. The quiet and unassuming town really did feel like a ghost town. Its silence and emptiness was eerie, but the marvellously majestic towering canyon walls in which it nestled gave it a somewhat surreal presence.

I anticipated a five-day hike in total: three days to the source of the river at the Mismi peak, and a two-day return to Tuti. I was to depart as planned on July 1st, after spending the preceding two days acclimatizing to the altitude, resting and sunbathing in the town square. I felt comfortable spending most of the day just sitting on a bench, letting my mind wander as I contemplated what lay ahead of me. I knew that the hike would present both physical and mental challenges, so I took full advantage of being able to just sit and warm up in the sun, envisioning what I would experience in the upcoming days.

The day before my planned departure I bumped into a municipal worker at the only restaurant that was open for lunch. She taught English to the locals and was pleased to have someone with whom to practice her English. I gradually steered the discussion towards gathering further information about the area and the peak to which I was heading. As with many conversations involving adventure, she first brought up some of the possible challenges, sharing with me how a couple had died earlier that year hiking the Colca Canyon. She explained that a solo, unaided attempt to reach the Mismi peak presented many dangers and urged me to find and hire an experienced guide. Despite her warnings, she was unable to elaborate on what other dangers I would encounter besides the cold.

After the Africa cycle, I had become accustomed to some trepidation from locals about travelling to certain areas, so took her information with a pinch of salt. She continued to insist that I should take a guide, but I explained that I had committed to do the journey solo and unaided. She didn't like the sound of this, saying that if I went alone I would not make it! I did not take her pessimism to heart, so I thanked her and left before I had to endure any more of it.

I had managed to pinpoint four GPS waypoints which marked the peak, a mountain pass, Camp One and Camp Two. I had found the GPS co-ordinates online and they were my only real source of guidance for navigation on this leg. I liked the fact that I would be making my way by following my own unique route and not being reliant on a map to keep me on a steady path, as this felt as close to true adventure as I could possibly get.

My accommodation in Tuti was a family's renovated home, where I was the only guest. The renovations allowed room for visitors, so the house was designated as a hostel. The owners spoke no English, but my basic Spanish and rough illustrations allowed me to convey my reason for being in the area and to share my desire to summit the Mount Mismi peak. The owners were just as concerned about my solo summit attempt as the municipal English teacher had been, and as soon as I realised that they were also apprehensive about my journey, I excused myself and went to my room. It was not that I denied the possibility of danger, as I was well aware that there would be challenges, but, regardless of the negative opinions and warnings, my path and objectives were resolutely set. Entertaining such discouraging views served no purpose whatsoever and I chose not to let them bother me.

I was up bright and early on Sunday, July 1st. I hadn't slept much, partly due to a bitterly cold room, but perhaps more so due to a racing, wondering mind. As I walked downstairs I noticed that the owner of the hostel, who also seemed to be geared for a hike, was waiting for me. After a brief and broken chat, I assumed that he had taken his own initiative and had personally appointed himself as my guide for the hike up the mountain! I did what I could to explain my reasons for solo travel, and that I would not pay for a guide whom I saw as unnecessary. However, he insisted on joining me and, as I realised that he was free to do as he pleased, we set off together.

From research and advice, the first landmark on the way to the summit was the big religious cross that stood on a rock mound overlooking the town of Tuti. My self-appointed guide and I followed a stone path up to the cross. The path then carried on all the way to another ridge. I was hoping that the path and the rest of the hike would remain this comfortable and as clearly marked.

Due to the language barrier, my companion and I did not talk much as we progressed on our route. He seemed content just walking along with me, while I spent most of the time filming and taking photographs, more so as the scenery improved the higher we climbed. Whenever we did talk, it always revolved around my diet, which was apparently very strange to him. He could not understand why I did not want to eat animals or animal products and found my explanations quite humorous. We both laughed heartily as we somehow seemed to find humour in our differing views.

By midday on the first day, we had reached the end of the stone path, which subsequently opened out onto a large grass plain where a few cows were grazing. To my delight, my guide promptly waved at me and pointed in the direction of another path up ahead. He had not wanted to be my guide after all. He had just wanted some company on the walk to see how his cows were doing! It would be a solo hike from here on, as originally planned. I waved goodbye and thanked him for his companionship as I headed for the small path towards which he'd pointed.

My rations for the daytime hikes were two oranges and two bananas, with a planned breakfast of oats and a cooked dinner of quinoa and beans. I was carrying over six litres of water, but knew that I would also be able to collect water from the glacial streams up ahead. The fruit meant that I could walk throughout the day without stopping for too long to prepare lunches.

I was making good headway and by mid-afternoon I had reached Camp One. According to my GPS, I still had two hours of sunlight, so I decided to push on, heading for Camp Two. As I walked, a barking border collie suddenly startled me. The dog came closer and closer so I decided to throw a stone in its direction to chase it off. My intention was to scare it rather than hit it. Fortunately this worked and as the stone landed nearby, I saw the dog scamper to a small rocky outcrop from which, to my amazement, a small man popped out. He began waving at me but I could not tell if it was a go-away or come-here wave, so I opted for the latter.

I approached him slowly and with a big smile to show that I only had friendly intentions, greeting him in

Spanish with a loud, "Hola. Cómo estás?" ("Hello. How are you?")

We seemed to be alone, except for some alpaca that I noticed he was watching on the other side of the ridge. For all I knew this was his property, so introducing myself seemed like the respectful thing to do. He was a friendly old man and we chatted for a while, although I could not understand anything he was saying! I had only acquired some basic Spanish, and he spoke in a dialect that was even more foreign to me. Somehow one manages in these situations.

The cold and dryness of the high altitude had taken its toll on the thin and leathery skinned man. His wrinkled face wore the brunt of the arid climate conditions, and his greying hair and unshaven stubble further indicated that he was very old. I couldn't believe how he was managing to handle the cold dressed in just a shirt, shorts and sandals, with a single blanket wrapped over his shoulders. I explained that I was looking for the most direct and safest route to Mount Mismi. I could clearly see the snow-capped peak in the distance but had no idea how to reach it because of the surrounding valleys. The peak was positioned on the edge of a giant horseshoe shaped mountain range, with a deep valley carving the middle out of the horseshoe. The gentleman proceeded to draw a clear map in the dirt, plotting the easiest route to the peak. It turned out that by following the GPS waypoints, I had actually been zigzagging up the mountain. I thanked him and departed with a warm double-handed handshake over his cold and bony hand.

By following his directions I decided to make my first camp just before the Camp Two GPS waypoint. I was making good time and set up my tent behind a large, lone rock on a sandy patch of ground. I knew that as night approached, it was going to get very cold, very quickly. I managed to whip up some quinoa, garlic and onion for dinner, and was in my tent by the time the darkness and cold rolled in.

I slept wearing all my clothes and was wrapped in a sleeping bag with an inner sheet. I had never experienced camping in minus temperatures before. That night I lay frozen in my sleeping bag with my numb toes keeping me awake most of the night. I had packed light for the adventure and all my equipment was geared towards the warmer jungle environments that I would reach at a later stage. I hadn't taken the initial cold nights into any real consideration as they made up only a tiny fraction of the adventure.

With a lack of any proper deep sleep, I was up at sunrise and all packed up and ready to go again by 07:00. The mornings were as cold as the nights, and it took much of the early sunlight hours to warm up the surrounding terrain, and me. Knowing I wasn't going to warm up anytime soon, I decided to get moving as soon as possible, and set off hungry. I would eat brunch later, en route.

I managed to keep to the path that the old man had advised me to follow. The route led me around the carved out valley, onto a small ridge and towards a pass that would take me onto a plateau. From there, it was a climb of the last few hundred metres to the peak.

At 10:00 I decided to stop and cook some breakfast. I used water from the melting glaciers and cooked a hearty breakfast of oats, quinoa and chopped banana. This was the perfect breakfast to give me a boost for the rest of the day's arduous hiking.

By the end of day two, I had made camp just under the pass. I was making good time and aimed to complete the hike in four, rather than the five days of my initial projection. From my camp, I could clearly see my route up the pass, onto the flat plateau and eventually to the summit.

Besides a few bird species, I had not seen much wildlife on the hike. The mountain was relatively barren and I suspected that the alpaca herds had chased away whatever species were indigenous to that area. However, as I was filming my video diary, I managed to catch some wild vicuña (Peruvian deer) on camera. I was amazed at my luck. The animal resembled an alpaca but had a light brown pelt and white underbelly. It was a beautiful creature and the sighting boosted my morale as I prepared for bed.

I awoke in the middle of the night with a numb feeling in my head accompanied by a throbbing headache, which I assumed to be symptoms of altitude sickness. When I was 16, I had attempted to summit Kilimanjaro, but had failed due to altitude sickness. On that occasion I was vomiting and delirious as the porters escorted me down the mountain. I was afraid that the altitude had struck me again, but this time I was alone and isolated with no porters to assist me. I resolved to try not to think about it too much, but the headache remained, as did the cold, resulting in another sleepless night.

As it started to get light the next morning, I discovered to my amazement that the headache had not been due to the altitude but that the cold had brought it on, along with the water bottle that was right next to my head, which had frozen during the night. I had been lying with my head on an ice block! I was somewhat annoyed that I hadn't noticed this during the night, but was simultaneously relieved that it was the cold and not the altitude that had been the cause of my headache.

I skipped breakfast again and took off for the summit, equipped with a first aid kit, two oranges, two bananas, a pack of biscuits, my cameras, satellite phone, GPS and PLB, all stuffed into a pair of wellingtons tied around my neck. Leaving my tent in position for the day, my aim was to make it to the summit and back in good time before sunset.

The weather was perfection, with a warming sun, not a cloud in the sky, and not a breath of wind. The stillness and beauty enhanced the tranquillity of it all. It was as though the peak was inviting me to come and marvel at its grand view of the surrounding land. The beckoning peak was always visible as I progressed towards it, making the navigating easier. However, once I cleared the pass and reached the ridge of the plateau, I was met with a new challenge in the form of glacial sheaths that were a foot high and half a foot wide, shaped like enlarged serrations on a jagged crocodile's tail. Breaking an ankle became a very real concern and in my complete isolation, I knew that I had to use the utmost caution in making my way over these mini glaciers as I edged tentatively forward towards the peak.

9

Summit

I was making slow but steady progress, remaining in a completely focused zone. As I drew nearer to the peak, I remembered to fasten my camera to my head in order to capture the last 10 minutes of the ascent and my anticipated jubilation at reaching the summit. I was fatigued and short of breath. The last 100 metres had taken just over 30 minutes of carefully measured climbing.

As I neared the peak, I could see that the side facing me was pure exposed rock face, far too vertical to climb. I was hoping that my chosen route would lead me behind the peak onto a flatter ridge, avoiding the exposed rock. I assumed that the path would eventually flatten out further so that I could then easily walk a few metres to reach the highest point and stand on the actual summit. This route would have me climbing in the shape of a fisherman's hook, straight up and then bending around the jagged, steep, daunting rocky face, eventually uniting me with the peak.

I reached what I suspected to be the top of the ridge and what would essentially be the end of my climbing. To my frustration, I was met with a 200 metre sheer drop on the other side of the mountain. The ridge of the expected summit was about 20 metres long but only a foot wide and was impossible to even stand on. I had come the wrong way! A knife-edged obstacle lay between my immediate goal and me. I could see the actual peak but it was impossible to reach! After all my efforts, what I perceived to be the last section and reaching what I thought would lead me onto the peak, only to be met with another challenge, filled my body with disappointment and I let out a disheartened bellow at the mountain.

I was resolutely committed to reaching the summit, as this would be the official start of the adventure, so I had no choice but to try again from the other side of the mountain. This would mean descending an estimated 100 metres, rounding the base of the peak and re-ascending, a further projected two hours of hiking to reach the true summit. Realising the narrowing time frame and supply constraints, I devoted myself to the task at hand and began my descent with a renewed determination.

I reached the base of the peak relatively quickly and rounded it by almost 180 degrees. I could finally see a clear route up to the official summit. Fortunately there were many more rocky outcrops on the re-ascent route, which allowed for convenient spots to rest and to gradually adjust to the high altitude. My shoes and pants were soaked from a combination of my body heat and the melting ice of the glaciers, so I resorted to swopping my shoes for the waterproofed wellingtons.

More appropriately dressed for the conditions, I plodded on carefully, focused on my goal. As I reached the peak, all my frustrations dissolved and standing on the highest point in that region I was captivated by the magnificent beauty that unfolded around me. I had clear, 360 degree views of the land, and could even see the curvature of the earth's surface. On this cloudless day, the beauty of the scenery was mesmerising. I remained quiet and still as I took it all in, breathing deeply and rhythmically in the altitude.

I was alone, with no other sign of human life near me, no planes in the sky, not a sound to be heard – just the natural architecture of all the forces that had shaped the land into what it now was. It felt as though I really was on top of the world, a moment that I will forever hold close to my heart.

All my previous challenges, as well as the cold and hunger, simply evaporated. I could understand how people could become so spellbound at successfully summiting any challenging mountain, and how they could become so enthralled by it all, that real life and the need to descend disappear. There are very few moments in which one has the opportunity to be totally in awe and humbled, not by one's own achievements, but by the achievements of something else – the beauty of Mother Nature's grand design. At just over 5 700 metres, this was the highest point I had ever reached. I was proud that I had done it alone, despite my inexperience and initial poor navigation.

I had promised Chanel and my mom each a phone call once I reached the summit, so I whipped out the satellite phone to share the moment with them. The conversations brought a wonderfully uplifting feeling as I sat mesmerised on the peak. I wished that I had someone there with me to share the experience, but the short phone calls were the next best thing. The intensity of emotions after the phone calls resulted in a few quiet tears as I sat alone on the glacial cap of Mount Mismi marvelling at the magnificence of our planet.

10

Back to Tuti

The initial false summit had used up precious time and I soon realised I'd have to get moving back to my tent to beat the cold and dark. I took a few more photos on the peak and then plotted the easiest route down. I began my descent just after 13:45 feeling on a real high from the successful summit and with the realisation that the adventure had officially begun. I estimated that I had less than four hours of sunlight left, so this spurred me on to make a rapid descent. I wanted to drop altitude as quickly as possible, mostly to escape the bite of the bitter cold. I made good time, and the descent to base camp took just over two hours. Since I had made such good time on the descent, I decided to pack up my tent and press on back down the mountain.

By 17:00 I had covered considerable ground and decided to set up camp in a small rocky outcrop that I hoped would protect me from some of the cold. It didn't. I froze again that night, despite having resorted to sleeping with all my clothing on and tucking my sleeping bag into my backpack. I could not handle much more of this piercing cold. From only three days of camping, the big toe on my right foot had become numb and remained constantly numb. I had also foolishly underestimated my food requirements, relying too much on the assumption that I would be able to cook the food I had brought, but the cold kept me hidden in my tent, as I did not dare to venture out to start cooking.

I was up early on day four, determined to reach Tuti by day's end. Yet again, I set off considering it too cold to prepare breakfast. With a better perspective of the mountain, gained from the previous few days climbing, I managed to plot a direct route back to Tuti with relative ease. The enticement of fresh fruit and a warm meal consumed my thoughts and kept me motivated to continue hiking with minimal food and rest. I could feel my stomach grumbling, but my desire to wait for some proper cooked food somehow subdued the urge to stop to set up camp and cook something to eat.

I could feel the fresh air filling my lungs on each step I took down the mountain. The altitude was dropping and my endurance seemed to be boosted by the apparent increase of air pressure that allowed fuller breaths. After eight hours of hiking, I reached Tuti and headed straight for the only restaurant that was open. I dumped my bag, placed an order and waited for some cooked rice, potatoes and a basic salad. Although very simple, at that moment it was a gourmet meal, and I savoured every mouthful, ordering a second helping shortly after I'd finished the first.

Despite the accomplishment of reaching the summit, and ultimately in a shorter time frame than expected, even with the slight detour, I knew that there was still much further to go. This was only the beginning. I headed back to the hostel and had a shower, washed my clothes and went straight to bed. Stage one had officially been completed.

The next stage was a cycle of an estimated 800 kilometres, during which I expected to experience more high altitude and cold. I decided to allow myself a day's rest and resolved to buy a blanket so I could keep warm through the coming nights of camping in the mountains. Thus far, the cold had been my greatest obstacle, and I'd learned from the hiking experience that a cold night and little sleep makes for a lethargic and arduous following day. I knew that I would not be able to afford any sluggish days on the bicycle.

11

The Cycling Challenge

The next morning I set off from Tuti on my bicycle. At an altitude of over 3 400 metres, it was the highest at which I had ever cycled. I was met by a steep gravel road that carved its way up the first of the many mountains I was still to cycle. The road snaked up the mountain like the coils of a tree boa wrapped around a branch, all stacked up on each other. My out-dated maps didn't even show this route, but a truck driver I had met at the restaurant in Tuti had assured me that it was the better and faster route to travel. However, he had neglected to mention that the roads were in a poor condition and that this was a short cut for a reason. My lack of route information, combined with the poor roads, high altitude and freezing conditions, made things extremely challenging and revealed just how underprepared I was.

The initial climb from Tuti and out of the Colca Canyon took five hours, most of which was spent pushing the heavily laden bicycle up the steep road. Walking the bike was extremely awkward and demoralising, taking its toll on my body. The going was tough and the bike would have to be perfectly balanced as I pushed, or it would have a mind of its own and go wherever its weight and gravity took it, either running away or falling on top of me. My muscles, especially those in my back, would cramp and I would have to lay the bike down, stretch, and then put all my effort into picking the bike up and getting going again.

In eight hours of 'cycling' on that first day, I managed to progress only 25 kilometres, with few breaks, and this poor accomplishment irked me. I felt like I was going nowhere, with the only real gain being one in altitude. I went into a negative state and was starting to despise my bicycle and doubt my abilities. I felt like the worst cyclist who had ever attempted to tour, especially since I knew that I was capable of far greater mileage in a day.

What seemed to be the only positive experience of that first day came near the end, when I arrived at a small truck stop inn that had a few rooms for passing drivers. I got a bed in the open dormitory and had a good dinner of potatoes, rice and a salad. Slightly despondent and still fairly frustrated, but suitably relieved to be warm and fed, I fell asleep, dreaming of eventually hitting the hot and living jungle.

The cycling did not get much easier. In the next week, I averaged only 35 kilometres per day, struggling along at high altitude on the constant climbs and testing descents. I did spot a few birds and the odd alpaca herd en route, but other than that the scenery was rather uninspiring. I eventually decided to discard the maps and resist looking at the mileage displayed on the GPS. Cycling roads that didn't exist on the map and viewing miniscule advancements in terms of mileage, forced me to abandon all forms of planning and mapping. It was gut-wrenching to see that after three hours of non-stop cycling, I had only covered 10 kilometres. I would have been covering more ground if I had chosen to walk. My bicycle became more of an unwanted burden than a worthy ally.

It then dawned on me that being self-critical and getting frustrated was not helping the situation, and was instead making it worse. So I resolved not to be so hard on myself, and resorted to simply following the road, accepting the circumstances and acknowledging, 'I will get there when I get there'. No more speculations, projections or objectives. I would simply take it one day at a time and dismiss any expectations or goals regarding daily progress with the cycling.

On day twelve I finally reached Cusco, Peru's second-largest city, a city steeped in history and tradition, and a gateway city to the renowned Sacred Valley of the Incas. I had cycled just over 400 kilometres and was fortunate enough to have had tar roads and relatively flat terrain for the final 150 kilometres coming into Cusco. En route, I had met up with into two other cycling tourists who

Cycling past the Egyptian Pyramids

Cycling through the Sudan desert

Rick & I reaching the Kenya/Tanzania border

66

Danger! Wild animals

Night cycling

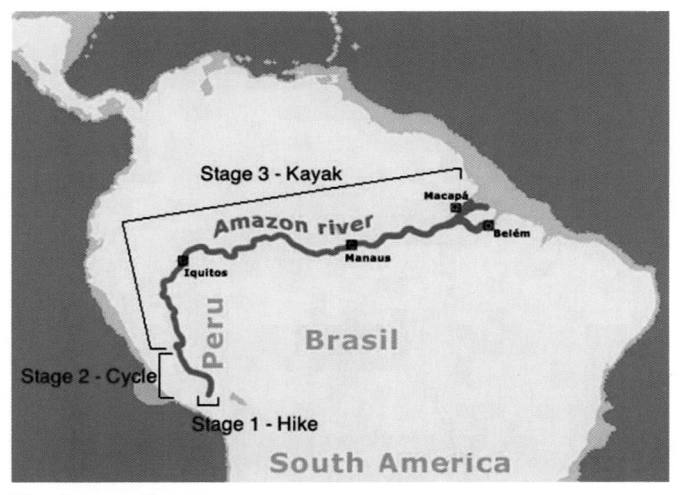

The Amazon Project map

My hosts in Tuti

Hiking Mount Mismi

Summmiting Mount Mismi

My first view of the Amazon Jungle

were also on their way to Cusco, having cycled from Argentina. The company, and the familiarity of speaking English, brightened up the final part of the cycle leg. After nearly three weeks of being alone, with no way of communicating or relating to the Spanish-speaking Peruvians, I was overjoyed to be cycling with two new comrades.

We cycled into Cusco together and as we got nearer to the city centre, traffic and community infrastructure increased. The hustle and bustle of Cusco forced us to slow down as we weaved through the overwhelming traffic. The couple knew of a good hostel that was a haven for cycle tourers and could be our rest for the night so we made our way there.

I was amazed at the number of cycle tourers who had gathered at this particular hostel. I met eight other tourers, mostly Europeans, all in the midst of their own cycling adventures. We spent the afternoon exchanging stories, sharing our varied cycling experiences, discussing touring bikes and comparing the essential equipment that each tourer relied on. I soon realised that my American-made steel-framed bike with no shock absorbers was by no means a luxurious touring bike, especially in comparison with the more stylish and reliable German-made models. My choice of equipment sure hadn't made the cycling any easier, and I realised that having the right equipment for specific activities can make the difference between carefree enjoyment and pure torture.

I decided to rest for a day in Cusco and after further discussions with the other cyclists, I spontaneously decided to change the route of my onward journey. A young German couple, who had just come from the route I was planning to ride, told me that the roads on that route were poor, the mountains high, and the going extremely slow. By that stage I was tired of poor terrain and slow going. I was way behind my schedule for the cycle, and I realised that I had to increase my daily mileage and find a more efficient route to the river. I had been cycling roads that followed the Amazon River's main tributary, the Apurimac, but due to the steep canyons and mountainous terrain, I'd very rarely seen the river.

Besides the slow going, the biggest issue I was encountering in Peru was the number of seemingly ferocious stray dogs scattered throughout the country-side. They had no fear, and would jump towards me, attempting to bite the bicycle, or me, as I rode past, regardless of the speed at which I was cycling. As soon as they spotted me, their barks would echo through the communities as if to alert the other dogs that there was a foreigner in their territory, and they would run at me, darting out of every alleyway! Out-cycling them was not an option, and what proved to be the best deterrent was to hop off the bicycle and walk alongside it. As soon as I stopped riding, the dogs paid no attention to me whatsoever.

Despite the harassment from the pestilent dogs, what bothered me the most was that the majority of them were strays and were clearly malnourished. It disturbed me to see so many neglected and abused creatures. I realised that the poverty of the communities seemed to reveal itself through the condition of the dogs. There were countless hungered dogs, digging in rubbish, looking for any morsel they could find. Humans had domesticated these creatures, forcing their dependence on us and we had then substituted the nurture for neglect. Seeing the many pregnant dogs also highlighted that the cycle of neglect was perpetual, ultimately just worsening the situation.

All the dogs appeared to have a red tinge in their eyes that made them look even more aggressive and menacing. While cycling a more remote part of the country, I saw a stray dog cannibalising another dog that had been run over. The dog just stared at me and as I stopped to hop off my bike, I noticed the red in its eyes. I then assumed the red tinge to be a symptom of disease spread as a result of cannibalism.

The large-scale cruelty and neglect I was seeing continued to trouble me and it took up most of my headspace while I cycled. I began to think of solutions to this situation, exploring the best possible ways of preventing the unnecessary cruelty to the helpless dogs. Education about the treatment of the animals, or kennels for the strays, didn't seem like viable solutions to the epidemic of neglect and disregard that often seems to be a product of poverty.

I envisioned establishing a business or organisation to create some kind of birth control pill which could be tailored for dogs and could end any stray dog's ability to reproduce forever. Such a pill would substitute the costly and labour intensive procedures of spaying or neutering. I could find a way to administer the pills to the stray populations, which would be a hassle-free and less invasive way of ultimately ending the continuous cycle of abused and neglected animals that are a by-product of inhumanity. A few generations down the road there would be no more of these dogs being neglected or abused. The pill idea kept me thinking daily, as I envisioned an end to not only stray dogs but perhaps the possibility of it evolving into a way to eliminate the need for the culling of other animals. Every time I saw a stray, it would distract me from cycling, and I would focus on all the angles of producing such a product.

Cycling through any country really provides a broader perspective of its animals and environment. Cycling through Africa, and Peru, highlighted the effects of poverty on animals. In Peru, the livestock seemed to have it the worst. Cows were often tied up to prevent them from roaming, chickens would be cooped up awaiting purchase, and pigs would be penned in tiny stalls, living in their own excrement. It was appalling to witness. While cycling through Africa I had seen people slaughter and chop up cows and goats and this always left a sick feeling in my stomach. Poverty seems to create the conditions that allow this kind of treatment of animals to be publicly accepted.

Seeing the appalling cruelty inflicted on these animals first-hand is heart-rending. No matter how much I try to understand it, there is never a viable explanation or excuse for inflicting cruelty on, or exploiting, any creature. Poverty seems to desensitise humans, affecting everything in its surroundings, including the animals, as though the continual cycle of hand to mouth living never allows the full development of compassion towards other individuals and species. It hurts the heart to see both humans and animals suffering due to the imbalance created by a capitalist-driven system. Poverty reminds me of the mass neglect in the world, how humans have become blind to each other's hardships and sufferings. Witnessing the effects of poverty on both humans and animals is, for me, the worst part of cycle touring and it always haunts me the most.

12

Jungle Calling

The new route I had devised would take me towards the world heritage site of Machu Picchu. I figured that because of Machu Picchu's tourism value, the route would be tarred and I could expect more sophisticated and tourist-orientated amenities. My predictions for the initial 150 kilometres proved to be spot-on: the roads were good, and I found some great eating spots along the way, as well as more modern, comfortable accommodation.

I managed to cycle just under 100 kilometres from Cusco and spent the night in Ollantaytambo. It was the most I had cycled in a day since starting the adventure. I had my first puncture as I rode into the town, but other than that I had a great day of cycling. Ollantaytambo, one of the gateway towns to Machu Picchu, was bustling with people from all over the world either embarking on, or returning from, their pilgrimage to the ancient Incan city. I considered making the trek or taking the train up, but decided that it would be an unnecessary detour from the task at hand. The jungle was calling me.

After a good night's rest and some extravagant beans on toast in the morning, I departed for the Abra Malaga pass, the final climb of the entire adventure. It was 50 kilometres of winding, steep road that rose from 3 200 metres to 4 600 metres, a challenge I had expected and for which I was ready.

The gain in altitude took me from the greener river-bank vegetation to snow-capped mountains and barren cliffs. The contrast in scenery was exceptionally beautiful and I took advantage of the many opportunities to look down from the various viewpoints on the ascent. I could see lines where vegetation ended and shrubbery began, and again where shrubbery ended and the barren rocky mountain walls began. By day's end I was just short of the pass where my descent would begin. I had started the day in shorts and a shirt, and finished in long pants, a jersey, a beanie and gloves.

I set up camp in a small rock enclosure, which I assumed was previously used for housing livestock at night. It seemed to be abandoned and looked like it would provide perfect protection from any wind that may whip up during the night. Although the extra blanket did make a big difference, it was still a cold night's sleep. I awoke to a layer of sleet and snow covering the tent and the surrounding land. Despite the cold, I knew that the worst was over and that in a few kilometres I would hit a long downhill, bringing warmer temperatures as I entered the jungle oasis.

I decided to skip breakfast and to either look for food on the way or cook breakfast later. I was nearly in the jungle and wanted to get going! By 13:00 I had reached the end of the pass and the final descent lay ahead of me. I would be dropping from 4 600 metres to just under 2 000 metres, 60 kilometres of pure downhill on an immaculate stretch of tar road with no pedalling required.

The mountain was covered in cloud and I could barely see 50 metres in front of me as I set off downhill. The persistent cold made my nose run and my eyes water. I stopped after a few kilometres at another small truck stop, deciding to head inside to warm up and get something to eat. Upon placing my order with one of the ladies, I noticed a plump guinea pig scampering past my leg and under the table. It was a pleasant surprise until I noticed that guinea pig was on the menu! I ordered tea and decided to sit outside by the bike, thinking it would be the perfect spot to do a quick video diary.

I mounted the camera on my handlebars and began speaking about the descent and the realisation that I was getting closer to the jungle. As I was recording, two giant condors surreally flew into the view of the camera. The few locals at the truck stop erupted with shouts of exuberant joy at the visiting condors. The locals clearly had a special relationship with, and a reverence for, these magnificent guardians of the sky. The critically

endangered condors were my first real sighting of wildlife in the past few weeks. My optimism was instantly
boosted, and I hopped onto my bicycle eager to get going
again.

Shortly after the condor sighting, I emerged from the
low cloud and saw my route unfold as it went winding
downhill through the jungle. Massive trees surrounded
the road, and the green array of the plant life was clear
evidence that I had finally reached the borders of the
Amazon Jungle. The high altitude and barrenness of the
mountains was over, and the dramatic change of scenery
signalled the promise of new experiences in a different
environment.

The more I dropped in altitude, the greener and
louder the jungle and its inhabitants became. Parakeets
and giant cicadas were the main instigators of the noise.
By day's end I was officially in the jungle, with just over
120 kilometres to go to officially complete the cycling
stage. The roads eventually turned back to gravel, but I
didn't mind, as I was finally in the hot and humid jungle
surrounded by ancient trees, a widening river and the
sounds of new and exciting animals yet to be spotted.

13

Time to Paddle

Five days after leaving Cusco, having completed the final 320 kilometres of the cycling leg, I reached Kiteni, where I'd decided my paddle would begin. Kiteni was a small communal town on a bend of the Urubamba tributary, which allowed for easy access into the water. The cycling stage had been just over two weeks of slow going, high altitude, bitter cold, steep descents, and steeper ascents, and sending my bike home could not have come soon enough.

The following day, I packed up my equipment and took a two-day bus ride to Lima, where I would send the bicycle home and collect the kayak before returning to Kiteni to commence the paddle. Stage two was finally completed. The long bus ride allowed time to reflect on the journey thus far and to contemplate the final stage of the adventure. It was with an excited, yet nervous anticipation that I realised that I would soon be paddling the mighty Amazon River. Despite the challenges I had overcome in the cold and miserable cycle, I kept reflecting on what I had experienced. I was continually looking for how I could use what I had experienced as a way to add substance to a retelling of the adventure when I got home. I felt as though my mind wanted to amplify parts of the adventure into dramatic and gripping titbits, worthy of exciting and entertaining those at home. 'Was I attempting this journey for the pure adventure or was it for the opportunity to share a story greater than my own personal ambitions?'

I was in two minds as to why I was in the jungle and what my priority was – a great story of man 'conquering the elements' and rising above the challenges, or something more personal, something that drew me even closer to the natural world and closer to an understanding of the heart and mind. I continued to ponder on my true intentions and came to the conclusion that I would allow the adventure to pan out as it was meant to, while choosing to rather focus on making it safely through each day.

I had spent nearly a month navigating my way through the Peruvian Andes and it was only on having completed the hiking and cycling legs that I started to feel that the adventure was truly beginning.

A projected three and a half months of paddling lay ahead of me. I had no idea what I would encounter. The jungle had just been a vision in my mind since the first day I had conceptualised the idea of navigating the Amazon River while cycling through Africa. All the time and effort of the past year was ultimately to get me to this point, paddling the mighty river, heading towards the Brazilian coast. My mind fluttered with doubts: 'Maybe I overestimated my abilities to actually paddle this powerful river? What if I don't make it to the end? What if I fail completely?'

Despite my apprehension, I committed myself to trusting in my abilities and realised that this would be the test of character that I was seeking. I was in the midst of the experience of a lifetime and it was providing all the challenges and rewards that I had envisioned adventure to offer.

14

Unprepared

From what I'd seen while cycling adjacent to the Urubamba tributary, the rapids on that part of the river looked fairly timid and relatively easy to navigate. As a result, my confidence began to grow as I felt quite capable of being able to handle these sections of the river. When I reached Kiteni, I thought it would be the perfect spot to begin the kayaking leg. I had initially planned to cycle a further 180 kilometres to link up with the adjacent Apurimac tributary. However, the heat, the tiresome cycling, the inviting water and my desire to begin paddling as soon as possible all convinced me, somewhat prematurely, to start paddling from Kiteni and on the Urubamba River, one of three main tributaries that feed the mighty Amazon River.

For the paddling leg of the adventure, I had settled on using a foldable kayak, consisting of an aluminium frame and canvas shell that folded away into two bags.

The foldable kayak made logistical sense as it was easier to transport and cheaper to post. It was a touring kayak, able to carry a paddler as well as equipment, but it was primarily designed for flat and open water. The rapids I had seen up to that point were predominantly Class I and Class II rapids so I assumed that the kayak would be robust enough to easily manage these seemingly small passages of white water.

A week after catching the bus to Lima, I returned to Kiteni. On the last connecting mini-bus trip back to Kiteni, I met an elderly German couple, Francoise and Gerhard. Being the only three foreigners on the bus, we got chatting, and we soon realised that we shared an interest in each other's business in the Urubamba territory. I explained that I was navigating the Amazon River from source to sea, highlighting what I had done thus far, and outlining my plans to paddle from Kiteni. I noticed the couple's apprehension and looks of concern as I spoke.

The conversation then took a turn as I listened to their reasons for being in the area. The German couple revealed that they had lost their son to the river 10 years ago. Their son (Frederic) and a friend had decided to construct a raft and float downriver from Kiteni to the Pongo de Mainique, a beautiful canyon where the water funnels through a break in the Peruvian Andes mountain range. The two friends had planned to raft 120 kilometres of the Urubamba River. Sadly, in one of the more challenging rapids, Frederic had fallen off the raft, had been pulled underwater, and was never seen again. This was not the kind of news I wanted to hear just before I was to set off on the same stretch of water. Worse still was that the couple then informed me that this stretch of the Urubamba Valley was known to be swarming with fully operational members of the Shining Path, a local terrorist organisation that had resurfaced in the region in defiance of the government.

Since I had been out of range of news for weeks, I had no idea about the state of affairs in the Urubamba area, or anywhere else for that matter. A month before I had reached the area, there was a reported kidnapping of 30 civil workers by the Shining Path from a town a few kilometres up river from Kiteni. I had been completely oblivious to the Shining Path threats, and had not encountered any hostility or unease in the area. The fear among the locals, which had emanated from the reported kidnapping, had never reached me. I resolved not to give it too much more consideration.

To commemorate the passing of their son, Francoise and Gerhard had established a sustainable agriculture organisation called 'Help For Peru' (HFP) in the Urubamba Valley, and they had been visiting the area regularly for the past 10 years to monitor its progress. They shared that the resurfacing of the Shining Path had led to strict military patrols and had resulted in enforced curfews throughout the Urubamba Valley. They told me that the fear amongst the locals was the worst they had ever experienced, and that this visit was the most dangerous time that they had ever spent in the region. Despite the chilling news of their son's drowning and the added threat of an active terrorist organisation, I was inspired by how they had turned tragedy into triumph through establishing the organisation that commemorated their son.

I had already cycled through the troubled area and hadn't experienced any problems or hostility. Being made aware of the Shining Path's resurfacing and the kidnapping incident didn't affect my perceptions of the area, although it did make sense, why all the towns were so heavily patrolled, including daily helicopter patrols.

I took what I could from the couple's precautions, mainly that the water was a lot more powerful than it appeared to be, and that precision in navigating would be critical. Their son's drowning did remain with me, and my thoughts began to shift as I questioned my judgment, 'Was my decision to start paddling earlier than projected short sighted and impulsive? How well prepared was I?'

Once back in Kiteni, I stocked up on a good supply of food, assembled the foldable kayak and took a day's rest to prepare mentally for the paddle. I had never kayaked a river of this magnitude, nor used a foldable kayak before. My only experience was some white-water rafting which I had done while still in school, but that seemed like child's play compared with what I was about to tackle. Acknowledgment of my inexperience provided a reminder to pay constant attention to the environment and the water, and to be particularly aware of getting to know the feel of the foldable kayak.

Despite some obvious apprehension, early the next morning I was on the riverbank, with the kayak afloat and loaded with all my equipment. As I eased into the river, I felt the kayak to be steady and buoyant, despite its load. It felt comfortable and very stable which was a clear confidence booster.

The Urubamba Valley comprised of steep, sheer mountain walls, painted with a green array of abundant plant life. The river flowed through the winding valley, summoning any extra water from adjacent streams as it made its way towards its merging with the mighty Amazon River. Since it was still the dry season, the water level was fairly low, leaving many exposed sandbanks in the middle of the river, with tall reeds sticking all the way out. During the cycling, I had been monitoring the water from a distant and higher perspective, constantly searching for a good put-in point for the kayak. Sitting in the kayak, afloat on the river, gave me a whole new perspective of the Urubamba Valley's amazing beauty, with its dark, brown-green water flowing gently between the vertical valley walls.

Kiteni was the only town on the water's edge that had a calm and flat entry point to the river. This was one of my main reasons for deciding to start paddling there, against the original plan of paddling the adjacent Apurimac tributary. However, now that I was on the water, in the kayak, I immediately realised that I had grossly underestimated the power and size of the Urubamba's rapids, as well as the fragility of the foldable kayak. I could feel the pull and push of the water bending the kayak as the inconsistent water started to become more unsettling.

The first rapid that I attempted instantly submerged and nearly capsized the kayak. I felt unprepared and out of my element in the powerful flow of the river. I considered finding some way to return back to Kiteni instead of attempting any further paddling, but realised that paddling upriver was near impossible, so turning back was not an option. Whether I liked it or not, the only way was onwards. I resolved that, given my predicament, the best option would be to walk the kayak downriver and to guide it through or past the rapids. I fastened a tie-down to the kayak's nose and floated it downriver as I walked alongside it on the riverbank. I knew how fragile the kayak's hull was and every bump and scrape sent chills down my spine. I had to proceed as carefully as possible while remaining vigilant at all times.

The river flowed in intermittent sections. Large parts of it were pooled and flat and I was able to comfortably paddle these parts, but every five to six kilometres, the large pools would funnel into smaller sections, creating the perilous rapids. I'd then have to get out and navigate these sections on foot, floating the kayak through the safest and smallest parts of the rapids.

As the day drew to an end, there was one more rapid I wanted to pass before looking to set up camp. I inspected the rapids from the right-hand river bank. From an elevated position, I decided that the left-hand side of the river looked to be the safest. It even looked possible to paddle and I decided I wouldn't have to walk the kayak through the rapids. All I had to do was make a hard paddle to the other side, about 50 metres away, from where I could then safely get through the rapid section at its calmest near the left bank.

I jumped into the kayak and began a hard dash for the other side. I figured I could use the water's increasing speed to get across the river more quickly, before reaching the white water. I was almost across when I felt the powerful undertow take hold of the kayak, pulling me downriver, sideways and towards the rapids. I realised I was not going to make it across in time. I needed to straighten up in order to enter the rapids head-on. I could feel the river dragging the kayak in different directions at will, yet I managed to keep my tracking direct and used my paddle and rudder to manoeuvre through the building white water.

Wham!

I went straight into a submerged rock and in the blink of an eye I was catapulted out of the kayak as it capsized. I was thrown out of the cockpit, like in a scene from a cartoon, where the unsuspecting victim is pole vaulted out of a vehicle that goes from moving to stopping in an instant. I tumbled around uncontrollably in the white water, and it felt like I was in a giant washing machine. The suddenness of the impact and consequential capsizing caught me completely off guard. I hadn't fully realised what had happened until I had already been sucked underwater. I felt the undertow of the water pulling me into its depths. I didn't have a life jacket on, as I hadn't brought one with me, not expecting to need one on the journey. Realising this short sighted and vital safety error, I held tightly onto my paddle, which I knew was securely fastened to the kayak, and hoped that it remained attached.

Eventually, to my relief, I felt the paddle leash tighten and I used it to pull myself onto the capsized kayak. Like a drowned rat clinging onto a piece of floating wood, I drifted downriver on the capsized kayak's hull and as the water flattened, I kicked to the side. I reached a small beach nestled in a rocky outcrop where I unpacked the kayak and then turned it over to drain the collected water.

Everything was soaked, including all my equipment and food, despite them being in dry sacks. I was startled and shaken, and realised that I was in way over my head. According to local knowledge, I still had more than 60 kilometres of rapids to negotiate before the river would be safe to paddle!

It was only day one on the river and I had almost destroyed my kayak, my only means of transport for the next 5 700 kilometres. This could have put an end to the entire adventure. I had also irresponsibly put my own safety at risk. I lambasted my impulsive decision to prematurely begin paddling rather than waiting for a more appropriate section of the river. I realised I would have to come up with a creative solution to get me out of this predicament.

I set up camp on the small beach and lay in my tent thinking about what I could do to ensure safe passage for the next 60 kilometre stretch. Kayaking was clearly no longer a viable option. I wondered if perhaps there was a road that followed the river, which I could run along to bypass the next 60 kilometres of white water. I was committed to doing every inch of the journey under human power, so taking a bus or motorboat downriver would equal failure.

Just as I started to relax and drift off to sleep, I was abruptly disturbed. I froze in fear when a man banged on the tent and blinded me with his torchlight. I had assumed that I was alone as I hadn't encountered any other humans that day, and hadn't seen any dwellings in the jungle. Fortunately he was friendly and had kindly come to offer me a blanket. He also asked if I was interested in some coffee at his house, which was hidden somewhere in the thick of the trees. I hadn't seen him at the time, but he'd seen me coming down the river and had watched me capsize. He'd obviously realised that all my goods were wet. His thoughtful gesture of offering me a blanket seemed very considerate, but I respectfully declined, as the humidity of the jungle was enough to keep me warm. I finally drifted off for a few hours and was woken by the rising sun and squawking parakeets.

As I was packing up camp, the same gentleman came to see how I was doing and kindly offered me some cocoa leaf to chew. Again, I graciously declined. We had an amicable chat as I packed up, and I explained my objective of navigating the Amazon River. He informed me that the next 60 kilometres of water leading to the Pongo de Mainique, what he referred to as just the 'Pongo', would be even more challenging in terms of rapids and that if I hadn't managed what I had just been through, I definitely wouldn't be able to handle that next stretch.

However, to my delight, he said that there was a small town just around the bend called Ivochote, where I could find accommodation and food. Since I didn't have too many other options, it made sense to head to Ivochote and then figure out how to proceed further from there. I was extremely grateful for the man's advice. He had provided valuable information and guidance just when I had needed some. I packed up camp, we bade our farewells, and I set off for Ivochote, hoping for an imminent solution to my quandary of how to proceed further.

I reached the small town just under an hour later and checked into a small hostel. The receptionist informed me that the roads came to an end in Ivochote. From here on, it was apparently just water, jungle and steep valley walls. So, the running option was out of the question.

I considered swimming as another option, as I have always been a strong swimmer. Growing up, surfing had given me confidence in my ability in the water. However, after thinking more about the story of Frederic's drowning, I realised there was no chance I would be willing to attempt to swim. My priority was to get through the 60 kilometres of white water with my kayak intact, and without doing any harm to myself. The river was the only way I could do this, so I had to figure out another way.

15

A Solution from Chico

I spent the next two days in Ivochote brainstorming and seeking a solution as to how I would navigate the small yet dangerous section of the river to ensure a safe passage for the equipment and me. It was a 60 kilometre stretch that could make or break the entire adventure. I could easily have hopped onto one of the large motorised boats, used as taxis, and arrived safely at the flat part of the river to re-commence the paddling, but this would have gone against the spirit, and my self-imposed rules, of the adventure. In the grand scheme of things, 60 kilometres in a 6 500 kilometre journey was a mere grain of sand on an entire coastline, minuscule in comparison to what I had already done and was still to do, yet my commitment to human powered transport compelled me to seek a viable alternative to motorised transportation.

I explored the village while gathering knowledge from various individuals in the small community, including the boat skippers, who sat waiting to transport passengers up and down the river. I enquired, 'Is there a road or path through the jungle to run on? Is there sufficient riverbank alongside the river for me to walk on?' The answers I received confirmed what the hostel receptionist had suggested, that the roads ended a few kilometres up ahead. Due to the mountainous terrain, paths were non-existent, and navigating through the jungle on my own seemed way too risky an idea, especially with the Shining Path threat, which was made evident by the heavily armed military patrol units stationed in Ivochote.

I had ascertained that the white water definitely ended at the Pongo, and that the river then became calmer and safer to paddle. However, up until the Pongo, there were several dangerous rapids flowing through the steep canyon walls, which also made walking along the riverbanks extremely challenging, if not impossible. I kept coming up against the 60 kilometres of dangerous water; only 60 kilometres that were holding me back from getting ever closer to the Atlantic coastline and my ultimate goal.

Late on the second day of wandering around the village, I surprisingly bumped into Francoise and Gerhard, who happened to have arrived in Ivochote a few days before I did. I explained my predicament and asked whether they were able to offer any possible solutions. I was initially reluctant to explain my situation, as I knew their son had drowned just a few kilometres downriver, and I was concerned that I may cause them to recall the painful memories of their son's passing.

Fortunately, Gerhard was open to a full-scale brainstorming session to see if we could come up with a solution to my challenging conundrum. We sat discussing possibilities over afternoon tea at the local restaurant. Gerhard's first suggestion was to ask one of the locals to construct a wooden balsa raft similar to the one their son had used to float downriver. It was a good idea, but it would require time and resources that I didn't have. I was also not prepared to cut down a few trees for a raft I'd use for just a few days. Furthermore, this option would probably mean another week's wait, which meant no measurable progress. Waiting didn't get me any closer to my goal. I liked to keep moving.

After much deliberation and bouncing around various ideas and options, we left the restaurant somewhat frazzled and no closer to a solid solution. I decided to go for a walk around the small town with Gerhard. I was desperate for any company, and Gerhard's warm demeanour and kind smile filled my longing for some companionship. As we walked around, engaging with some of the locals who benefited from the work of HFP, we passed a mechanic's shed. A tiny squirrel monkey sitting on a tyre immediately caught my eye. I made a beeline for the fascinating little creature and as I got closer, it noticed me approaching and proceeded to run straight towards me, up my leg and onto my head, where he began scratching for lice, bugs, or whatever he thought was living in my unwashed hair! Gerhard decided to continue on, as I told him I would like to stay and spend some time bonding with my new sidekick.

Eventually the mechanic came out to speak to me, and as the monkey quickly ran to him, I realised the critter was his pet. The mechanic introduced himself as Manuel, and told me that the monkey's name was Chico. I carried on chatting with Manuel, practising my Spanish while Chico hopped from him to me, and back. A solid hour passed, as we intermittently chatted about football and played with Chico. I was so captivated by the curious creature that I completely forgot about finding a solution to navigating the next 60 kilometres of the river

While having a fun time with Chico, I noticed a large truck tyre lying on the floor of the shed. Immediately, I thought back to the time when a few friends and I had floated downriver on tyre tubes. That was it! A tube suddenly seemed like the perfect solution! Floating on a tube would be slow going, but it would allow me to navigate the river under human power. Even though I had previously tubed down a river, I had never done it on this scale, and I realised that I was going to need the largest tube available to keep me safely afloat.

Unfortunately Manuel didn't have any extra large tubes for sale. He said that the only place I might be able to find one was a few hundred kilometres upriver, at the slightly bigger town of Quillabamba. I was enthusiastic about this new solution and the idea of tubing the river, so I thanked Manuel, bade farewell to Chico, and headed back to the hostel to make plans to get to Quillabamba.

Luckily, there was a daily bus to Quillabamba, so the following day, I made the eight-hour ride to the town. Once there, I easily managed to find and purchase a large truck tyre tube, big enough to support my weight floating down the river. I spent the night at Quillabamba and was back in Ivochote the next day.

Once equipped with the tube, I began to finalise my plan. I speculated that the river was flowing at a steady five to six knots and figured that ten hours of floating would allow me to complete the sixty kilometres in a single day. I would reach the entrance of the Pongo, find a place to camp for the night and wait to catch a boat upriver the next morning. From there, I would collect the rest of my equipment at the hostel, head back to where I had finished tubing, and then start kayaking.

I hadn't in my wildest imagination envisioned that I would be cruising down one of the main tributaries of the mighty Amazon River on a truck tyre tube! However, as daunting as it felt, my apprehension was being side tracked by the realisation that this was not only the best solution, but that this would also add to my story. Adventure was not about everything going according to plan and this was the proof. I had adjusted to my changing environment and formed the analogy that while it would be a completely new experience, it would be an example of literally 'going with the flow'.

I was up at 05:00 the next morning. I'd spent five days planning and waiting, and I was eager to get underway. I ate a small breakfast of fruit, went back to Manuel's shed to get the tube inflated, spent a few minutes playing with Chico, and then made my way to the river. I had attached two tie-downs to the tube, giving me two places to hold on, and tied a third securely around my waist to substitute the lack of a safety jacket. I used my tent bag as a backpack, in which I placed the inner shell of my tent, a poncho, my PLB, a camera, three oranges and two bananas. These were the bare essentials that I assumed would sustain me for at least a day.

I was exceptionally nervous as I waded into the river with the tube. I would make sure that I would always keep close to the riverbank, and if the opportunity arose, I would walk along the bank rather than float in the water. I knew that the longer I waited the greater the fear would become, so I resolved not to hesitate any further. With a small amount of trepidation and a giant leap of faith, I hopped onto the tube, and floated into the flowing waters of the Urubamba River.

16

River Tubing

By 06:00 I was well on my way and floating steadily downriver. I had already seen some big fish displayed at the various food markets, and had also heard that the river otters tended to be quite territorial, so I did whatever I could to keep as much of my body as possible out of the water at all times. After an hour of floating I started to become more confident and more at ease with the idea of tubing. As I started to feel comfortable, I relaxed and turned my focus to the beautiful surroundings and the indigenous sounds of the jungle.

The vegetation was incredibly dense, creating a solid wall of green leaves and thick brown trunks. Some of the bends in the river cut into the jungle walls, leaving the trees to hang over the water's edge, forming a temporary umbrella from the sun. The sounds of parakeets squawking their uncensored greetings, the buzzing of giant cicadas, and a whole host of other birds and insects singing their morning calls, all formed a beautiful natural symphony that filled the humid morning air. All the creatures making a noise, seemed to have a structure and rhythm to follow; or perhaps each one was sending a message into the jungle, waiting for a response, and then answering back. The giant cicadas were by far the loudest. Depending on how I positioned my head, their sound would either amplify or drown out, but the recognisable steady humming of the cicadas vibrating their abdomens was always present.

It was like being in a busy market where everyone is talking at once. It seems noisy, but when you pay attention to specific conversations, you begin to decipher and understand the jumble of noise, and are able to interpret the many individual conversations going on at the same time. This was the jungle's morning conversation. Each creature had something to say and share, and it did so confidently and rhythmically. Each unique species seemed to have its own set of communication skills and was participating in its own form of discussion with the others.

The great green of the jungle and its giant trees seemed so foreign in comparison with life at home and in the city. I felt dwarfed as I drifted along the river between the adjacent jungle walls, alone, on just a tube. The initial trepidation had dissipated, and in the few moments of sitting and taking in as much as I could, I realised that this was where I was supposed to be: not floating down a river on a tube as such, but on an adventure in the unknown and with a mission to encourage the protection and conservation of the natural world. This feeling of knowing that I was in the right place for the right reasons resonated deep within and produced a real sense of contentment and bliss.

My actions had resulted in my merging with the incredible and wondrous life of the jungle, reinforcing my reasons for doing what I was doing. I felt humbled and privileged to be floating down the river all alone, surrounded by the jungle and the symphonic creatures singing their unique melodies.

Just as I was starting to get used to the diverse attractions of the sights and sounds of the jungle, the time came to attempt my first rapid on the tube. I prepared by positioning myself on my stomach, while gripping the two straps, so that I could use my legs for kicking and steering. This first rapid was fairly small, but I quickly realised the tube's poor manoeuvrability. I got stuck in a small whirlpool and was spun round and round like a record on a turntable. I decided to see if I could swim out of the eddy, but as I lowered my legs into the water I felt the powerful pull of the undercurrent, prompting me to quickly hoist myself back onto the tube. Fortunately, the pull of the water on my legs had managed to result in the tube being nudged out of the whirlpool, and I continued to float downriver.

I was relieved to have gotten through the maiden rapid, but it dawned on me that I was too inexperienced to be floating along on a massive, unpredictable body of water like this. It had been a relatively small rapid, but it had shown me that perhaps a tube was not the best option for navigating the dangerous rapids. I resolved to float on the slow-moving water and find a way to walk or climb around the more menacing rapids.

At about midday, I noticed the small, inquisitive face of an animal peering at me from a small rocky outcrop. I had been constantly scouting for animals and before I could guess what I had seen, the animal dived into the water. I instinctively took my legs and arms out of the water. The animal's head then popped up just in front of me, and I realised that it was an otter. The otter did a few laps around the tube as it eyed me out from a distance. It seemed cautiously interested and was possibly trying to work out whether I was a threat or not. As soon as it realised I wasn't, it returned to its little crack in the rock to dry off, catch some sun and sleep. It was a rare sighting. The supposedly territorial creature seemed pleasantly surprised by this larger foreign creature floating down the river on a big black tube!

The encounter with the otter provided some welcome respite from otherwise tedious going. After a few hours of floating, I started to feel that the sun was taking its toll on my exposed skin. The backs of my legs were tight, sensitive and raw. Being in complete awe of the jungle had resulted in me taking my focus off my body, and the slow going added to the hours of roasting in the tropical sun. I had already managed to portage several rapids, and started to believe that the tube had been, after all, the most appropriate option for navigating this section of the massive river.

As the day drew to a close, I sensed that I was getting closer to my destination. The riverbanks that I had walked on during the earlier portages had transformed into steep canyon walls. I could hear the daunting roar of the tumultuous white water ahead as I floated nearer towards the narrowing passage through the canyon. I could eventually see where the Pongo de Mainique officially began. It appeared just as it was described: 'a geological crack in the mountain range that narrows the flow of the water into a tiny gorge'. From the noise being generated by the imminent rapids, I realised that they were far too massive and dangerous for me to attempt on the tube.

The vertical walls leading up to the Pongo were full of an almost luminescent, deep-green moss and intricate, fragile cobwebs, as very little sun reached into the canyon. It was eerie, but I figured that attempting to climb along the scary and damp-looking walls was a better option than risking tubing the rapids. I clung to the rocks as I pulled myself out of the water. I tied the tube around my back, and must have looked like a ninja turtle as I began climbing along the steep walls.

The moss and trickling water from above made the rock walls slippery, and the cobwebs proved to be the nests of giant rain spiders. I figured that a potential duel with a scary spider was a better option than taking on the powerful white water and risking drowning in the river. I climbed slowly, taking my time, finding solid footholds and reliable handgrips as I edged myself towards the entrance of the world renowned Pongo de Mainique.

While I was climbing I unexpectedly noticed a plaque with an inscription on it attached to the opposite wall. It was dedicated to Frederic. This was obviously where he had disappeared, and looking at the tumultuous water below, I could see how easy it would be to get sucked under by the current. There were also probably many underwater caves, and once you were in one of those, you would never come out. Seeing the sign was a reminder of the dangers of the area and it made me grip the wall even more intensely.

With a few metres to go, I was challenged with my final hurdle, as the walls became far too steep to climb. The only options were to go through the water or to backtrack and climb the canyon by taking another route. I wasn't prepared to backtrack 15 metres of horizontal climbing and then have to find another route, so I decided to lower myself into the water, sit on the tube and pull myself carefully along the wall to avoid being sucked towards the rapids.

I lowered myself gently into the water and sat upright on the tube, gripping small holes and cracks in the rocks to pull myself along. As I gripped one of the crevices I startled a massive rain spider, easily the size of my hand. It fell onto the tube, and I immediately froze! If I let go of the wall to try to brush it off, I could lose my grip and get sucked into the rapids. I decided to endure the spider's presence as I slowly made my way around the small jutting piece of canyon. Fortunately the spider remained still, and as I safely rounded the wall and landed on a small beach, I gently brushed it off and it scuttled away. I had finally reached the entrance to the Pongo de Mainique!

After just under 10 hours of floating, walking and climbing, and with painful sunburn and an empty stomach, I had reached my destination. As I scouted to find the best place to set up camp for the night, I suddenly noticed three young fishermen just ahead of me. I had been so preoccupied with rounding the small canyon wall that I hadn't previously seen them. I thought it would be best to introduce myself to avoid any possible hostility. From a distance, I shouted a friendly, "Hola!" ("Hello!") I proceeded slowly towards them with an outstretched hand and a broad smile. I was met with a warm response.

We got chatting and I learnt that they were from a community based upriver and had come to the Pongo, as it was the best spot for fishing. The pooling of the water into the narrow gorge made for easy fishing, as the fishermen simply dropped a net into the gorge and the currents would literally sweep the fish straight into their awaiting trap. I offered one of my oranges to them as a gesture of friendliness and goodwill, seeing as we would be sharing the same campgrounds for the night, and they gladly accepted the token.

I noticed a small beach nearby on which I decided to set up camp. I assembled my tent and returned to the riverbank to chat to my new friends. They were all brothers, aged 10, 14 and 18. I felt like a true foreigner when I saw their shelter for the night: they had fashioned small trees into an igloo shape, lay a plastic cover over the structure, then added more leaves as further insulation. My tent now seemed like a luxury dwelling in comparison.

I shared the relevant details of my adventure with them, how I had come to be there, and what my plan was. They informed me that I could catch a boat upriver in the morning, to reach Ivochote by midday. Exhausted, I thanked them, said goodnight and headed for the comfort of my tent for a well-deserved sleep.

By sunrise I had packed up camp, and was sitting on the tube waiting to catch a ride on one of the passing boats. The oldest of the brothers came over to offer me some pasta and one of the fish they had caught during the night. I had only eaten two oranges since the previous day, as my bananas had turned to mush while tubing, and throughout the night I had felt the emptiness of my stomach. I was famished, but declined the friendly offer of food. He asked why and I told him I did not eat fish, or any other animals. He thought it was slightly peculiar, but seemed to accept and understand my reasons.

Two hours later, I managed to catch a boat upriver and I was back in Ivochote just after midday. I was tired, hungry and sunburnt. I stopped for a quick lunch of salad and rice and then headed for the hostel to get some rest. I was exhausted, but was feeling positive, enthralled by what I had just accomplished and content with how I had risen to the challenge of navigating the daunting rapids on the tube. The following day, I would officially begin paddling towards the sea, my final destination.

17

This is the Amazon Jungle!

Early the next morning, feeling well rested, I boarded one of the motorised commuter boats with my equipment in hand. I asked to be dropped off at the small, exposed beach at the entrance to the Pongo that I had camped on after tubing the river. Once there, I began assembling the kayak, contemplating what lay ahead. It dawned on me that this still felt like the beginning of the adventure, and that I still had a very long way to go. Despite this realisation, I was excited to finally start paddling on the calmer waters, imagining all the rare jungle creatures I would see along the way.

I envisioned encounters with river dolphins, trees full of monkeys, maybe a mighty anaconda, or perhaps even the elusive jaguar coming down to sip from the water's edge. These visions and fantasies filled my mind until I had finally assembled the kayak and edged it slowly into the water. A massive journey lay ahead of me. All the planning and preparation was about to come to fruition as I eased into the kayak and started paddling down through the Pongo de Mainique.

The steep walls of the Pongo channelled the river into a long alleyway. The canyon walls allowed only minimal sun exposure, and the sun would only reach the river when it was directly overhead. Yet all along the Pongo, different plant species found the smallest areas of exposed rock onto which to attach their roots and hang down towards the water below.

The canyon walls stretched almost 20 metres up into the air, with a width of 10 metres at the widest sections. It was as if I was paddling down a city side street, between two huge skyscrapers, the only difference being that these walls were covered in a variety of vegetation. Isolated waterfalls and streams cascaded down the vertical walls. Every now and then, a bird would fly from one side to the other, only visible for a brief moment as it flew directly overhead, before disappearing between the walls of the Pongo.

Once through the Pongo de Mainique, the jungle terrain flattened out into a large basin with only a few rolling hills visible in the distance. It was just reaching midday and the sun seemed to reflect the green of the jungle onto the water, giving it a deep viridescence. The trees stretched high into the air above the waterline and formed an impenetrable treetop canopy. From a distance, it seemed as if I was paddling on a cloud of trees, but as I got closer to the plant life, I became dwarfed by its magnitude. The jungle was so thick that I could only peer a few metres into it before it became a mesh and maze of plants.

A few towering trees stood regally as they pushed through the canopy. These colossal trees were covered in hanging vines and seemed to be the wisest life forms of all the jungle. A few bare-trunked palm trees shot straight through the canopy, tall and skinny with a burst of distinctive leaves right at their tops. I had no idea that palm trees could get that tall, and soon realised that the jungle is ruled by its plant life – the governing force of the Amazon. The plants have no limits to their growth. Water and soil nutrients are in abundance, so plants compete only for sunlight, constantly growing upwards to reach out and grab as much of the sun's rays as possible. I felt a surge of elation as I gazed around, marvelling at the lattice of plants sharing the jungle floor. I thought I had reached the jungle a few weeks earlier when I entered the Urubamba Valley, but realised that I'd only been on its outskirts and was getting closer to its heart.

Before the Pongo, the jungle was like a tame potted-plant garden, while after the Pongo, the plants owned the land, and the mighty river I was paddling on was their reliable stream for getting the water they required to thrive. The jungle stretched in all directions to the horizon. I was a lone paddler cast adrift in a sea of plants and trees, with only a water path to navigate my way.

This was the Amazon Jungle! This was what I had envisioned and had come here to experience!

I had been paddling slowly as I was taking in the new sights and diverse sounds, but the slapping of my paddle on the water was distracting me from truly absorbing the indigenous sounds, so I decided to stop and take it all in. The cicadas were on an all-time high, their vibrations ringing through the jungle at an incredibly high pitch. The birds seemed to have quietened down in the middle of the day, but their presence was still gently heard. Perhaps the heat and humidity of midday forced the birds to tone down their chatter, yet the whispering of the huge flocks still murmured through the jungle walls.

I soon realised that my chances of spotting many of the exquisite indigenous creatures during my paddle would be rather slim. I was like an ant in my new environment, engulfed by my surroundings. Finding any rare Amazon animals would be like finding a colourful needle in a green haystack. The jungle was just too encompassing. The only real chance I was going to have of spotting any creatures would be if they walked, slithered, flew or swam directly into my line of sight. I reminded myself to really appreciate any new creatures that I would have the privilege of encountering.

I continued to paddle throughout the day, without stopping to set up for lunch. Being in such awe of my new environment had resulted in hunger being subdued. I used the kayaking time to focus on my paddling technique. I wanted to adjust to the kayak and fine-tune my paddling style to maximise comfort and performance. A good paddling technique, when one expects to be paddling 60 kilometres a day for over three months, is essential and can make the difference between decreasing one's efficiency and risking injury or increasing one's efficiency and preventing injury. I needed to drive from my core and make sure that I paid close attention to each stroke and to the feel of my body as I sliced the blades of the paddle through the water.

It was still my first day so I didn't expect to cover much distance. When I decided to check on my progress, I reached down for my GPS to check the mileage. I searched for it but it was not there. I remembered that I had paddled through a small rapid earlier in the day, and assumed that the splash of the water into the cockpit had washed the device overboard. My only remaining source of time was the clock on my camera and that would lose track of time when the batteries died. With no GPS for the rest of the journey, it would mean 'proper' navigating, and judging the time of day by the sun and humidity.

As the sun progressed on its daily arc towards the horizon, I decided to start scouting for an area to set up camp. I assessed the terrain on the riverbanks to see if I could find a suitable location. I wanted to be as hidden as possible to avoid unnecessary attention from any locals, although I had not seen many people on the river that day, aside from the odd boat passing by. After almost an hour of scouting, I finally noticed a small beach protruding from the wall of trees. I beached the kayak, surveyed my surroundings and then began to set up camp.

I knew that the most crucial part of adapting to the paddling and the new environment was to settle into a daily routine, most importantly a camping routine – a routine that I could use to measure my productivity and performance each day, and that would also allow me to notice any irregularities. Setting up and breaking camp needed to become second nature; knowing where all my equipment was packed in the kayak needed to become intuitive. Efficiency and speed were vital. I had to know how long it took from finding a camping spot to having camp fully set up, with a meal prepared and eaten. I also had to be able to break camp and get paddling again as quickly as possible and at any time, in case of an emergency.

I had to know the ground I was camping on, whether there were any holes or dens that may also be home to venomous creatures. In the Amazon, even some of the ants are poisonous. I had to be close enough to the water's edge to be in a position to break camp and get paddling swiftly, but not so close that the natural rise and drop of the river could sweep me off in the middle of the night. These were the foundations of an efficient and successful camping routine.

The sky looked clear as I started to set up camp, so I decided to sleep with just the inner mosquito netting shell on the tent, leaving the waterproof cover off. I had seen a boat just upriver and suspected I could be on the boat owner's land. If I was, I wanted to be able to see straight through the mosquito netting to notice if anyone was approaching during the night. I rustled up a light dinner of quinoa and rice and was in my sleeping bag as darkness set in.

Expecting some respite from the cacophony of daytime sounds, I was only met with a jungle that livened up at night! The raucous sounds kept me awake for as long as my eyes could stay open. I would hear crashing through the trees, instantly waking me up with a shock of adrenalin coursing through my veins. I would shine my torch into the jungle to see if I could spot anything significant, but never did – all I saw were small eyes reflecting in the torchlight. This happened several times on that first night. I was on edge and my sleep was interrupted. I resigned myself to the realisation that this was probably how I was going to be sleeping for the next few months, interrupted, and on the alert for any sound or movement.

At one stage I managed to drift off into a slumber, but I was woken again, this time by a dull roar that echoed through the sky. I felt drops of rain. The rain went from spattering to pouring in a matter of seconds and I hastily covered the tent with its waterproof shell. I had neglected one of the most important, yet obvious elements of the jungle: rain. I was in a rainforest, after all, and even though it was the 'dry season', I should have known to always expect the possibility of the heavens opening with a downpour.

The morning light slowly lit up a rainy, cloudy day. Due to the gloom of the clouds and the lack of sleep, I packed up camp sluggishly. I then cooked a small breakfast of oats and kiwicha (a local grain also known as amaranth, which was one of the staple foodstuffs of the Incas) and set off expecting a damp day on the river. The rainy weather did not alter much in terms of the surroundings. The chattering creatures were as loud as they were during the sunshine, and the humidity was as sticky as the previous days. Every creature and plant had adapted to the rain. I was the only organism that seemed out of place as I paddled in my rain jacket through the showering walls of water, with dull thunder mumbling in the distance.

The river seemed to widen progressively as I paddled. The main waterway of the Urubamba consisted of large, sweeping turns and bends that never quite straightened out as they carved through the dense plant life. I had seen aerial photographs and videos of the waterways and had noticed how they slithered through the jungle like the coils of a side-winding snake. The main waterways had smaller tributaries, which in turn had tiny sub-tributaries. The water channels seemed to resemble the circulatory system of the body, with the waterways being the arteries, veins and capillaries of the jungle, spreading throughout the jungle floor, interconnecting and ultimately ending up in one large water channel: the drainage of almost two thirds of an entire continent's water supply ending up in one large river, the Amazon River.

I had marked four stops on the map that would serve as the main rest and resupply points on my 5 700 kilometre paddling journey. Assuming that I paddled a minimum of 50 kilometres per day, the first rest stop would be Atalaya, a projected 12 days away. From there, it would be a further two-and-a-half-week's paddle to Pucallpa, followed by another two-and-a-half weeks to Iquitos. I'd break up the final seven to eight weeks of paddling by stopping at Manaus in Brazil, and lastly at Belem, just before reaching the Atlantic Ocean. If I found any other stops along the way, I'd consider them a bonus, but wouldn't rely on them. The estimated time it would take to reach each of the stops that lay ahead put the massive distance I still had to cover into perspective.

I decided on a regular routine of paddling between 07:00 and 17:00, with these 10 hours being the maximum time I would spend on the water on any given day. I would eat a substantial breakfast, paddle through lunch and have a hearty dinner. I was comfortable that this eating plan would ensure that I had sufficient sustenance during the long paddling days. At each resupply stop I would buy as much fresh fruit and vegetables as possible, providing my primary food source. Once I had depleted the fresh food I would return to living off the staple dry foods of quinoa, rice, oats, kiwicha and beans, all of which required cooking. My priority was reaching the checkpoint stops, so each day, paddling would involve using the daylight hours to get as far as possible to ensure paddling a minimum of 50 kilometres per day. The river was still flowing at approximately four knots and I estimated that eight to ten hours' paddling would easily see me reaching my daily goal.

Throughout the day's paddling, tiny flies, barely larger than a pinhead, relentlessly attacked. The incessant black flies would swarm in pockets in the jungle and on the river. If I got just close enough for them to sense my presence, I would be swarmed over. Perhaps it was my body heat that attracted them. The unfortunate thing was that I only noticed them once I was already being bitten, and by that time it was too late. Besides the initial sting, the flies would leave extremely itchy bites that would flare up every morning and evening. I would spend a good ten minutes just before I started paddling each day and again before I fell asleep, scratching my bare bitten body in the tent. At times I wanted to rip my skin off, and I would only feel soothed once I had scratched my skin raw and applied my insect repellent that contained a bit of alcohol. The alcohol would sting the raw skin even more, but would at least leave it numb and temporarily soothed. The pestilent flies and their bites were the worst part of each day. Nothing ever seemed to deter them.

The flies disappeared as the sun set, but then, like clockwork, they seemed to hand over to the night shift, as multitudes of mosquitoes would take over. These swarms were immense and their daunting buzzing could be heard from quite a distance. If I shined my torch through the mosquito netting at night, in a matter of seconds, the dense swarms of these buzzing barbarians quickly blacked the torchlight out. If I happened to roll against the side of the tent in my sleep, they would bite through the base layer that lined the tent. Even once I was in the tent and relatively protected, the continuous buzzing made it feel as though the blood thirsty tyrants were just a few centimetres from my face, and I was often taunted to the point of slapping and waving the air to shoo the imagined predators away. They were a true terror of the night!

As the days passed, I gradually became accustomed to my ever-present insect adversaries, as I began to settle into my routine and the environment, adjusting to a life on the river. I started to feel that my performance and endurance were increasing steadily day by day. I became accustomed to the feel of my kayak as it moved smoothly through the water, and I had developed techniques to keep more comfortable while sitting for long periods. Small adjustments in body position prevented my back from cramping and my buttocks from numbing on the kayak's seat.

Initially, I wanted to experience the true isolation of the jungle, so adhered to paddling the first 10 days without listening to my iPod or engaging in any forms of outside communication. After that first 10 days of solitude however, I reached a breaking point. The loneliness was inescapable in the isolated and vast jungle. I would see fishermen now and again, but it was mostly just my mind and I paddling down the river. I was starting to feel a mild depression set in and I felt that I was losing sight of the adventure. I began to miss the comforts of home terribly. Although I had attempted the challenge of loneliness and done quite well, I realised that I was starting to jeopardise my ambitions with my thoughts of instant gratification, so I finally decided to introduce my iPod into the scenario and began including listening to audio books and music as part of my daily routine.

I was typically up at first light, and would eat breakfast, and have camp packed by 07:00, making sure that I was on the water by no later than 08:00. I would spend the first two hours of the paddle speaking to myself and vocalising my thoughts about future adventures or about life in general. Around mid-morning I would listen to my iPod, most often audio books. I had several audio books on a range of topics, including some by various 'self-help gurus', but my favourite at the time was 'The Ricky Gervais Guide To...' series. I would immerse myself in the trio of comedians' frank and open discussions, as they provided not only great humour, but also the feeling that I was part of their conversations.

Depending on the humidity of the day, I would stop paddling around midday, find a comfortable position in the kayak and attempt to get in a brief nap as I drifted slowly down the wide river. After about half an hour's rest I would return to paddling. During the afternoon, I would listen to music to keep myself motivated to push through the last bit of paddling for the day. Around 16:00, I would start looking for a suitable location for a campsite. Camp would be set up by 18:00 at the latest. My first task was to boil the river water that would be my drinking water for the next day. I would have dinner eaten and be in the tent by sunset, just before 20:00.

If I was still cooking in the dark, I would be bombarded by the mosquitoes that swarmed like bees at a hive. The light of my head torch would attract other bugs to fly directly into my face or into my food if I was busy eating. On one of the nights, while cooking, a giant moth slammed into the side of my face. Based on its size and the impact, I had initially assumed it to be a bat, and was so startled that I left my food for the night to seek protection in my tent!

Locals, mostly fishermen, woke me up on several occasions during the nights. If I hadn't woken up before they reached my tent, I would be rudely awakened by a shining torch in my face as their way of getting my attention. Fortunately, all of these encounters were as a result of them being inquisitive rather than hostile. I would explain my reasons for being in that region and they would eventually walk away satisfied, leaving me to get back to sleep.

I eventually decided to buy a machete, mainly for the purpose of eating coconuts, but also because it seemed to signal status and presence among the locals. Every night I would sleep with my machete, pepper spray, PLB and satellite phone right at my side as a precaution while I gradually adjusted to the unfamiliar territory.

My mind was constantly searching for necessary excerpts from each day of the adventure, parts that could add to my story. I would journalise every day's events, while occasionally sending messages via satellite phone to my mother, both as a way of assuring her of my safety and also so that she could add content to the website. It was almost as though I was viewing myself from the perspective of a potential moviegoer or book reader, as though my experience in the jungle was just a fictional story for a greater audience. My mind was the scriptwriter and director, constantly looking for angles to excite the viewer. I often felt as though I was jeopardising my own experience at the cost of how I believed someone else may wish to hear of my adventure in the jungle.

With regards to the Africa adventure, the first question I was often asked was 'What went wrong?' Everyone seemed to enjoy and thrive off the drama within adventure. Knowing this, my mind was becoming swayed into seeking the more dramatic events on the river. I was losing sight of why I had entered the jungle in the first place – it was for an incredible experience and not for things to go wrong. I pondered, 'If I had planned in order to eliminate the wrong, why was I searching for it?' I carefully monitored my intentions and constantly had to recheck my ambitions.

Since I was collecting data for Adventurers and Scientist for Conservation (ASC), I would ask the fishermen who I encountered for information about their catches. I would take note of the fish they had caught, snap some photos and then record the information in a journal so that I could eventually relay it to the organisation. The fishermen were the only real source of knowledge about the creatures of each region. I photographed fishermen holding up giant catfish, some of which would make slightly intimidating grunting noises! One fisherman had a boat full of piranha, and I was reminded of the potential dangers of falling into the water in the wrong place! Aside from the fishermen's catches, I hadn't seen much other animal life on the river. Even the birds seemed to be disappointingly scarce, hidden somewhere deeper in the jungle. I could hear them, but just never had the opportunity to spot the immense flocks of macaws and parakeets I was hoping to see.

A few more weeks passed, but my animal encounters and sightings remained scarce. The river dolphins were the most common creatures I began to encounter. I enjoyed the presence of these friendly greyish-pink river inhabitants as their inquisitive nature was rather endearing. I would hear a quaint popping sound as they intermittently surfaced to take a breath of air through their blowholes. Many of the dolphins frequently trailed along in the small wake of my kayak. I was really enjoying and appreciating their regular company until, one afternoon, an overzealous dolphin swam right under me and breached. I felt the kayak bend upwards as the dolphin pushed both the middle section of the kayak and me off the water. I got a real fright and went into complete shock. It seemed like such unusual behaviour. Luckily the kayak remained intact and I was relieved that I hadn't been toppled out of it.

I decided from that point on to be very mindful of the dolphins, and to paddle closer to the riverbanks instead of paddling in the middle of the wide river, so that even if one of the dolphins mistakenly managed to capsize the heavily laden kayak, I would be closer to land. It seemed like the safer and wiser option to keep as close to the riverbank as possible. Little did I know that the breaching from the dolphin and the resulting decision to stick close to the riverbank would soon prove to be life saving.

A real highlight in terms of animal sightings, came one evening, when after finishing cooking dinner, I decided to rinse my pots and machete in the river water. It was already getting dark, so I required my head torch to light the way. As I reached the water's edge, I waded about ankle deep into the water and began scrubbing off the rice that had stuck to the pot's base. The light from my head torch illuminated a small portion of the river in front of me. Suddenly, in my peripheral vision, I saw a snake slithering through the water and into my path. I stood completely still and felt my entire body tense up as the snake stopped right between my legs! After initially being startled, I began to relax and was amazed at the snake's behaviour, seeming almost pet-like as it proceeded to swim around my legs. After a few moments I felt comfortable enough to gently push it away, and dashed to grab my camera to snap a few shots for ASC. The snake was a little smaller than my arm and its beautiful and distinctive patterns identified it as a juvenile anaconda. I was incredibly invigorated by the experience and absolutely delighted that I had intimately encountered one of the Amazon's most renowned creatures.

A few days later, while searching for coconuts in the jungle, I came upon a massive, black snake. It was easily over a metre long and nearly as thick as my arm. The giant serpent rose up, cobra-like, and for a few tense moments, we both seemed to freeze in each other's presence. It tilted its head and for a long few seconds stared penetratingly at me with its beady black eyes, before it slithered off into the jungle. Unexpectedly spotting any different creature always gave me a boost, leaving me intrigued about what I might encounter in the days and weeks to come.

As I progressed further, the river continued to widen. With it being dry season, the benefit of the broadening river was that many sandbanks were exposed in the middle of the river, forming large enough islands to set up camp. Even though I may have been rather conspicuous when camping on the sandbanks, I would have a clear 360° view of my surroundings. Anyone who approached me would have to do so by boat, which meant I would hear and see them before they arrived. Camping on the sandbanks was more pleasant because the soft sand allowed a comfortable night's rest, and the sounds of the jungle were not as loud as they were on the riverbanks. The exposed sandbanks also had little insect life and very few mosquitoes, which was a huge relief. It was the most protected camping I could find, so sandbanks became a priority when looking for a good spot to set up camp.

Despite the few unsettling night time visits from locals, and the sometimes startling encounters with the various creatures, throughout the adventure I had felt relatively safe and undisturbed. The monotony of paddling day in and day out was a challenge but not the challenge I had envisioned I would experience in the Amazon. After some weeks on the river I found that I was adjusting to my new lifestyle and routine, but something in the back of my mind kept reminding me that it was becoming too easy an adventure. Everything seemed to be going according to plan, either I had planned too well or, like the African experience, the unknown parts of the world were perhaps not as dangerous as they were portrayed.

My mind started to become preoccupied with doubts. Every day that passed without any major challenge started to feel as if something was compounding, as I started to think that perhaps I was having it easy now because something more challenging was going to happen later, something untoward to make up for the easy days on the river. I scared myself at the thought that something bad was going to eventually happen and hoped that the negative thoughts entering my mind would remain just thoughts, and nothing else.

Before the adventure, I had envisioned a fantasy of stepping into a scene from a National Geographic Amazon Jungle showcase. I believed that I would be entering a jungle that was vibrantly teeming with life, and I expected daily encounters with some of the Amazon's most beautiful and rare creatures. Although I had been privileged enough to have a few such encounters, as the days and weeks passed, I realised that my grandiose fantasy would probably remain unfulfilled. The anticipated abundant animal life of the Amazon either seemed to be hiding deeper in the jungle, or their scarcity was due to the human factor. My focus shifted to analysing the human impact on the jungle and I began to take note of the changes that humankind had induced on the natural environment. Perhaps people really were the reason for the lack of monkeys and other wildlife one associates with the Amazon Jungle.

I had initially taken the green abundance of plant life as a reason to assume that the jungle was a thriving metropolis of nature, untouched by humankind. However, once I started to become more aware of my surroundings as a whole, and learned which signs to note, my perceptions began to shift. The further I travelled, and the longer I spent on the river as I made my way through the jungle, the more I began to notice that humankind's impact on this natural wonder was not a positive one. I was reminded that deforestation and destructive agricultural practices were real threats to the natural biodiversity of the Amazon region.

The visual signs of human interference with the jungle became apparent when I passed several huge, floating barges of large felled trees. The tree corpses were cabled together and fitted with propellers on each side to guide the floating graveyards down river to their final destination where they would probably end up as furniture. People seemed to value these giant trees more highly as consumer products than as living jungle organisms. The living trees supported so many jungle creatures, and it deeply hurt me to see these decapitated giants being floated down the river in such numbers. On each barge, an entire family seemed to have constructed a small settlement of tents that would house them on their journey downriver. It was fascinating to see how a family could have a temporary existence on a floating barge of logs, but it left me saddened as I realised that they were responsible for the deaths of the trees on which they floated.

Many a time, I witnessed large clouds of smoke billowing out from the jungle. These fires signalled the burning of endemic forest, which was to be substituted for agricultural land. The fires were burning more often than not, scattered throughout the dense jungle. Again, I found it so unfair how humankind could destroy whatever it wanted, for profit, and how the fate of the jungle was determined by the commercial value that humankind attached to it, and not by its biodiversity and the life it supported. I found it bizarre that the land was considered more valuable as agricultural land than as an essential natural phenomenon.

On one occasion, I had an interesting encounter with one of the locals living on a tree barge. I paddled up and moored my kayak to the barge, with the intention of initiating a friendly conversation and to see what information I could gather. As we got chatting, the father asked if I knew his friend, 'Edward from Britain'. 'What an absurd thing to ask', I initially thought. He seemingly assumed that every foreigner knew every other foreigner. 'Had he not realised that the world was a lot bigger outside of the jungle?' I paused for a moment, and it then dawned on me that he was probably talking about Edward Stafford, a British adventurer whom I had read about during my research for the adventure. Ed had managed to walk the entire length of the Amazon River, along with a local guide. It struck me how isolated this local man was from the outside world, and how isolated I was in this part of the jungle. This man had only ever met two outsiders, and both of them were on source-to-sea journeys of the Amazon River.

I often heard the dreary drones of chainsaws and the muted mooing of cows echoing through the jungle, sounds that were completely alien to that environment. The thick jungle walls hid the parts of the jungle that people had chosen to exploit. From my kayak, I could only see a few metres into the jungle. Almost daily, I witnessed double-rotor helicopters flying overhead, transporting huge pieces of commercial equipment. 'What could they possibly be building in the jungle?' I was too immersed in the great jungle to know what was really going on in its heart. However, the things that I did witness, proved that humankind had reached these isolated areas and was exploiting them for a profit. It frustrated me to learn that humankind was taking part of the last remaining natural world and was beginning to tear it apart, scarring it so badly with wounds that many in the outside world would never even know about.

It began to make sense why my fantasy of spotting all the beautiful creatures of the Amazon rainforest was not being realised. People had come in and started hacking at the Amazon's heart. Each tree cut down, each creature killed, had a ripple effect on not only the jungle, but on the planet as a whole. Here, on the main and most commercial part of the river, I was experiencing this effect at its worst. Life was being destroyed at the capillary levels of the forest, a destruction that would move to its veins, and infect its arteries. Paddling its main artery, I knew that a jungle that had taken millions of years to evolve was potentially on its way to being destroyed in a few generations. 'Why is this being allowed?'

Will we collectively only realise humankind's impact when it is too late, when the flowing green hills of trees have been substituted with rolling agricultural pastures in the pursuit of greedy green wads of money? It took me weeks of living in the jungle to notice humankind's impact, and I was one of very few individuals to have had this opportunity. I realised that the Amazon was being barbarously butchered for industrial profit. I had read reports and heard the facts about the destruction, but seeing it first-hand really struck a deep chord. I began to wonder what entity would allow such a destructive creature to exploit and destroy at will. What gives humans the right to attach value to and destroy the natural world as we see fit? I was bonding with the plants, trees, and local wildlife. Every fire I saw, every tree floating down the river, every chainsaw echoing in the forest, meant destruction, unnatural destruction. The premature death of one tree alone was enough to signal tragedy for the jungle.

18

Choosing To Live

As I lay slumped in the mud, surrounded by the thick jungle vegetation, I ran over what had just happened to me, as if trying to figure out whether my current situation was just a dream or a frightening reality. My bodily sensations confirmed that this was real. I had been shot and could feel holes in my body. I could taste blood in my mouth and I knew that I was critically wounded. Even though I had managed to flee the attackers, I knew that I was in one of the more isolated parts of the Amazon Jungle with nowhere to go and with no real sense of direction to follow, besides the river. All my equipment had been left behind in the kayak and the only people in the area were the ones trying to kill me. I had passed the point of desperation, feeling overwhelmed and utterly hopeless.

The more I questioned my situation, the more I realised that the odds were entirely and completely stacked against me. I was isolated and needed help, yet there was no one to provide any help, and even if there was help, how would I find it in the middle of the Amazon Jungle? The reality of my predicament only added to the negativity that tainted the possible outcomes I envisioned. I could feel negativity chopping down my internal pillars of strength and optimism, as I was trying to resist the notion that I was going to die from my injuries. It would be a slow process of bleeding until eventually my body would lose the ability to hold onto life. I began to speculate that my last few moments of life would be filled with a painful end, full of fear and suffering – I was going to rot and die in the Amazon Jungle, scared and all alone.

The enveloping despair was accompanied by the physical feeling of sinking deeper and deeper into the mud. Both the physical environment and my mental attitude were pulling me downwards, taunting me to accept the finality of a miserable death. I was suffering, not at the thought of death itself, but instead at the thought of the manner in which I would die.

I was caught in an internal struggle where my desire to live was fighting against the pessimism and reality of the dire situation I was in. The defeatism was taking over, creating more vivid ideas of just how miserable and painful my death was going to be. I envisioned myself lying in the mud for hours, fading in and out of consciousness, as I slowly died from blood loss and exhaustion. I didn't want to die, but reality painted the grim picture that death was an inevitable result of my overwhelming predicament.

Negativity, the enemy to my existence, pushed and pulled until it reached a saturation point and I concluded that death no longer seemed to be such a miserable option. I started to embrace and welcome death, acknowledging the reality that being dead was better than trying to figure out what to do or where to go. I reasoned that at least if I died I wouldn't have to endure the long term pain and fear I would have to face in the impossible task of finding my way out of the jungle.

The internal discussion then moved to the amount of pain and fear I could potentially endure. I thought of the pain I would experience if I wandered through the jungle with exposed and gaping wounds, desperately seeking a way out, and I imagined how fearful I would become as the sun set and the darkness brought out the creatures of the night. It would be a true living nightmare and I concluded that finding a way out would be filled with more suffering than if I instead opted to just lie still on the riverbank and wait a few hours before I bled to an inevitable death.

Out of the blue, I instantaneously hit a mental turning point, when it suddenly dawned on me that I had spent the last few minutes trying to justify a reason to give up living. I was denouncing my will to survive because of the potential pain and fear I may experience. I had spent much of my younger years reading, learning and working on developing a strong and resilient mind, yet now when I needed it most I was ignoring the fight within me! I felt out of character, as I was allowing negativity to have such a debilitating hold on my actions. This was not me and these were not the core traits that I wished to embody. I wanted to at least put up a fight. I had come face to face with death and had almost allowed it to get the better of me, but had decided that I would no longer submit myself to its strange appeal.

I recalled how simple breathing techniques can alter one's physical and mental state, so I began to focus on my own breathing, taking in deep, slow inhalations and exhalations. I was beginning to feel a resurgence of life as I awkwardly picked myself up from the mud and stood tall. I felt like a new human being and was capitalising on the internal shift and the realisation that no one but me was going to get me out of this situation. My breathing felt tight and weak, but I continued to take slow deep breaths and began collecting my thoughts.

'Okay, you have been shot. You are all alone in the middle of the jungle. You need to do something.'

I was becoming more rational in an attempt to comprehend my situation. As I stood on the riverbank, scrounging my thoughts, I began to seek motivation – motivation to live. I started to think, 'Why had I decided to run from my attackers? What had caused me to run in the first place?'

I started to feel life streaming back into my body and mind. I internalised that I had chosen to run out of a combination of fear and the desire to live. Fear had served its purpose by evoking a fight or flight response to the attack, but now that I was safely away from the attackers I had to think with more clarity, free from the influence of fear. If I had wanted to die, I would have stayed on the riverbank as the men continued to shoot. I didn't want to die – I wanted to live.

I continued internalising a more positive approach and began looking for ways in which I could remain motivated. I focused on creating a reason as to how I could rise to the seemingly impossible challenge that lay ahead of me. 'Perhaps this is the story I had spent the last several years seeking. This is why I had chosen to pursue adventure, for the unpredictable and character building moments, maybe this was one of them, maybe this was the challenge I had been yearning for and maybe this was the external situation required to test my internal nature.'

I held a reverence for all life, including my own and I resolved that every living cell and working part that was still keeping me alive deserved any opportunity and chance to live. I made a firm decision in the moment that I would not give up and that I would no longer wait to die. I would do whatever I could to keep moving, keep breathing, keep living and finding a way out, and the only time I would stop or give up would be if I blacked out from blood loss or exhaustion. As long as I was conscious and breathing, I would keep moving and searching for a way out of the jungle.

I had made a resolute decision to live and was fully committed to doing whatever I could to stay alive. If I died, it would not be because I wanted to die. I was not going to give up. The person who had closed his eyes and waited to die on the riverbank no longer had a say in my future.

I knew that my best chance of finding any source of help would be to remain on the banks of the main river, in the hope that a boat would eventually come past. I had to make sure that I was visible to any passing boats, and that I was able to attract their attention. I had a plan of action and realised that I could not remain still - movement signified living and I wanted to feel alive. I decided to continue heading downriver, always moving, always breathing, always positive.

With a renewed sense of purpose, I pushed on for a few hundred metres, walking and jogging lightly, following the bend of the river. I then took another moment to stop, assess and catch my breath. As I scanned my surroundings, directly across the river I suddenly noticed two figures emerging from the jungle. I could not believe what I was seeing. I felt that I may actually be hallucinating. I stared a bit longer and then realised that the men on the other side of the river may actually be my attackers. However, I quickly assessed that one of them was wearing a red shirt and the other a brown shirt, whereas the shooter was in a yellow shirt while his accomplice wore a brown rain jacket. They were not my attackers!

I briefly contemplated that even though they were not my attackers, they may be from the same community, so may also be dangerous, but I quickly realised that I had no other choice but to trust that they were there to help. Out of nowhere, two men had popped out of the jungle, directly opposite me. It was surreal. There was no visible community in this area and the river had been largely unpopulated for the duration of that entire day. 'Where had they come from?' I froze for a few moments, not knowing what to do. 'Do I shout for help or wait a bit longer to assess the possibility of these other two men as being potentially hostile?' Out of pure desperation I instinctively decided to shout out to get their attention, hoping that they would be able to help me.

I first tried to exhale a loud wolf whistle, but nothing came out. I tried several more times, but a shortness of breath left me blowing nothing more than a short peep of a sound. I then attempted to scream to them but again I could not make much of a noise. I was unable to build up sufficient internal air pressure to make a loud enough call or whistle.

I was starting to regain full movement in my left arm and decided to put every bit of life I had into a loud combined shout, wave and jump; one comprehensive effort to attempt to attract the attention of the men. I gave it my all and then collapsed into the mud to rest. I had very little energy and my breathing was worsening, which was making the calls ineffective. After several diminishing attempts, I had still not managed to capture their attention. I whimpered in the mud for a few moments at the thought of seeing potential help but not being able to do anything to get to it. It was so close, yet felt so far.

I was starting to feel hopeless again; hopeless that these men may not see me and that they would simply disappear back into the jungle. It was like living in a truly frustrating nightmare. I was doing my best to scream and shout but no sound was coming out.

One thought remained and dominated my awareness: 'I can't give up.' I convinced myself of my will to survive and recommitted to my decision to live. I was going to do whatever I could to get through this. I decided that if the men couldn't hear me, I would go to them. Somehow I would get across the river. My right arm was still locked but my left had regained almost full movement. I scoured the riverbank for a thick log or any other possible flotation device. I couldn't find anything, so I decided I would swim, using my legs and left arm. I started to wade into the water, but waist deep, I hesitated, 'What about the dolphins?'

Out of all the possible concerns I could have in the moment, it was the thought of the river dolphins that caused me to hesitate. I was concerned that if they were in this stretch of water and I was in the middle of it, their curious nature may lead them to start playing with me, which could result in me being pulled under the water. Swimming was not a good idea so I retreated back to the shallows and decided to attempt one more scream and jump.

As I took a deep breath to attempt a giant scream, I noticed that the two men had hopped into their boat and were pointing at me! I started throwing my left arm around, jumping and signalling. They had spotted me! They had finally noticed me and were coming to help!

Immensely relieved, I waited patiently as the men steadily made their way across the river. However, just as I started to think that I was about to be rescued, the men stopped abruptly about 50 metres away from me. They stared as if I was an alien from another planet. They didn't seem to want to come too close, but came close enough to see what and who I was. I made my hands into the shape of a gun and pointed at my head, signalling that I had been shot. I didn't know the word for 'Help' in Spanish ('Ayudar'), so I just shouted, "Por favor!" ("Please!")

They watched as I again gestured that I had been shot, and pointed upriver to show them where it had happened. I was then given another shock as the men proceeded to turn around and head back towards the other side of the river! I was completely flabbergasted at them turning around. 'Where were they going? Had they not understood that I had been shot and needed help?'

One of the men then turned to face me and put his hand up, indicating that I should wait there. I'd been acknowledged, and decided to do as I was told. Perhaps they were going to help me after all.

The two men made it back to the other side of the river, where another two men emerged from the jungle and climbed into the boat. The four of them then came back across and signalled for me to walk 20 metres or so downriver, to where their boat could come in close enough to reach me. The river at that point was too shallow and too muddy for their boat. The mud was almost a metre thick, which made my progress extremely slow and difficult. The four men stared at me in complete bewilderment and shock as they waited for me to make my way to the boat. They had probably never seen a foreigner on this part of the river before, let alone one in my bloodied condition.

I waded into the river and as I reached the boat, the men lifted me gently under my arms and into the boat. I flopped down, drained of energy, and just wanted a rest in the comforting safety of the boat. I was enormously relieved and lay there with an immense sense of gratitude towards my rescuers.

We headed back across the river and as I raised my head to see where we were going, I noticed several other people emerging from the jungle, awaiting our arrival on the riverbank. Once we got there, the men gently lifted me up and cautiously helped me out of the boat.

A woman suddenly started screaming and shouting. I must have looked like I had just stepped out of a battle scene or horror movie and the sight of me was clearly disturbing. My face was painted in blood and my body was smeared with mud. I had been drooling and spitting to get the taste of blood out of my mouth, so the front of my T-shirt was covered in blood and spit. The woman's reaction highlighted the seriousness of my condition. She eventually calmed down and two of the men held me under my arms, keeping me upright as we made our way into the thick jungle.

19

Now What?

The small entourage of locals took turns in supporting me as we followed a narrow well-trodden path through the dense vegetation. The surge of adrenalin and shock that had initially kept me going was beginning to subside, and I started to feel immense pain in my right shoulder, as well as throbbing in my back and neck. The hearing in my right ear had gone, along with the feeling on the right side of my face. I used my left arm to hold my right arm in a sling position, as a way of avoiding the pain I felt when I let it hang down and swing as I walked. I was becoming very sluggish so two of the men from the boat walked by my side and provided support. My legs felt like they were carrying an immense load and seemed like they wanted to cave in under me. I was carefully guided through the thick walls of the jungle until we reached a small village hidden among the tall trees.

I was surprised at the sight of the infrastructure that had been built in the middle of the jungle. I had not seen any civilisation from the river, as the network of trees concealed any signs of community life in the jungle. The small village consisted of several A-frame housing units, elevated just over a metre off the ground, each having one or two tiny windows. The houses were well-constructed and resembled small garden sheds or wooden cabins, all on stilts. Some of the dwellings even had porches in the front. Each abode had a small ladder for reaching the front door. There were also several larger structures that probably served as congregation points, perhaps a communal hall and a school. I was amazed at the advanced construction of the units. I was expecting mud huts or small concrete enclosures, similar to the informal housing I had seen in Africa, but here, hidden deep in the jungle, was an established and functioning village.

We continued through to what seemed to be the central congregating area. I could not believe how many people lived in this tiny community hidden away in the jungle. There were children playing football and people walking around or gathering to chat. All the inhabitants were dressed in tattered and worn western clothing. It was not how I expected a rural community of the Amazon Jungle to appear. The grass had been trampled and the passages between the homes were solid mud paths, similar to the pavements of a city. Looking up, I saw a clear view of the sky with a border of trees. It was as if the village was built in a small hole, with trees as boundary walls. The only way of knowing there was a village there, would be to fly directly over it and see it from the air.

The entire community understandably seemed to stop and stare as I was ushered to an open area with wooden benches, covered by a large palm-thatched rooftop. It was one of the very few structures that wasn't on stilts and it reminded me of a large bus stop or waiting area. Within a few short moments, the whole community, from young children to the elderly, surrounded me, as I was helped to sit down on the bench. The intrigued onlookers gathered round, wide-eyed, some whispering to each other, most just staring silently, as I hunkered down, tired and drained. When I left my head hanging for too long, my neck began to hurt, so I stiffened up my posture and looked directly ahead of me, staring zombie-like at the curious crowd.

A man came over to me with a cup and insisted on me having a drink. However, I was sceptical about what I may be drinking as I thought it could be traditional medicine that may make me hallucinate. I refused to drink as the man held the cup against my lips.

"Que es esto?" ("What is this?")

"Agua con azucar." ("Sugar water.")

"Solomente agua con azucar?" ("Only sugar water?")

"Si." ("Yes.")

Accepting that it was only sugar water, I gulped the cup's contents down. The sugary solution took away the bitter taste of blood and immediately woke me up from my zoned-out, dazed state.

I attempted to start self-diagnosing my condition. My initial sense was that my back had huge gaping wounds from the impact of the shots and that my neck was blown open. I decided against touching the shots' entry holes, as I was scared that if I felt a big hole in my body I might start to panic. I assumed that the numbness in my face and loss of hearing in my right ear were symptoms of a brain haemorrhage caused by the shots to my skull.

As soon as I internalised that I could be suffering from a brain haemorrhage, I immediately started to worry about my thought patterns in the fear that I may lose control of my ability to think of a way out of the jungle. The belief that I was experiencing a brain haemorrhage instantly began to distort my perceptions of reality. I started to feel separate from my body and as if the situation was not real. I began to think in the third person and felt very alien to my own situation.

'What must I do?'

'What would Davey do?'

'I bet Davey would be surfing.'

I felt as though I had lost control of my own thoughts and was becoming nonsensical, which strengthened my belief that I must have a brain haemorrhage and that it was making me delusional.

I was distracted from this mind numbing thought pattern by a diminutive elderly woman with long, grey, straw-like hair. Her face was wrinkled and she was by far the oldest woman I had seen in the community. She approached with a bucket of warm water and a sponge, sat on the ground beside me, and started wiping the dried mud off my legs. I was in such a daze that I just stared blankly at her as she continued to clean my dirty body. As soon as she touched me I sensed a level of acceptance and greater calmness from the other villagers. It was as if she was acknowledging that I was not so foreign and that it was acceptable to help me. Her action seemed to have dispelled any illusion of separation.

The left side of my throat was punctured, making swallowing difficult. I could taste blood in my mouth and just allowed it to drool into my lap rather than painfully swallowing it. The caring woman gently continued to wipe me down until I was cleaner. It was the compassion and kindness of the old lady that provided a temporary sense of calm as I sat on the bench, confused and separate from my own existence.

My thoughts then moved to the concern that I may be bleeding from the wounds in my back. I decided to try and sling my shirt around my back and chest to cover and apply pressure to the holes. As I took off my shirt, a few people behind me gasped, which alarmed me, so I put my finger to my lips to silence them. The energy required to tie my shirt was more than I could muster, so I resorted to letting the shirt hang loosely around my neck and shoulders.

Every time I attempted to do something, I would first ask myself, 'What am I doing and why am I doing it?' Just taking off my T-shirt had caused an internal discussion about why I should take it off in the first place. I was thinking so strangely and my thought process was so foreign that I felt like I was going insane. I could not do anything without talking to myself to evaluate what I was doing. To move a part of my body, I would have to internally instruct that part of my body to move.

Another woman took her cue from the older lady and started cleaning the dried blood off my back, lifting up the loosely hanging shirt as she dabbed around my wounds. I felt her cleaning several different areas on my back and could not comprehend why she was cleaning so many different areas. I'd counted only four shots. 'How could four bullets have caused so many isolated and scattered wounds?' I wondered.

I closed my eyes and started to think.

'Okay. You need a doctor. Now, how do you say 'doctor' in Spanish?'

I looked at one of the men near me.

"Tiene usted un medico?" ("Do you have a doctor?")

I was met with no response.

"Tiene la medicina?" ("Do you have medicine?")

Another man stepped in and answered. I could not completely understand what he was saying but got the gist of his answer. They had no doctor, nor basic first aid kit, in the village. Every time I spoke, I had to take a deep breath, and could only mumble the words. It required huge strength and effort to talk, so I decided against talking unless I had something really important to ask or say. I knew that the town of Pucallpa had a hospital, so asked, "Cuántas horas al Pucallpa?" ("How many hours to Pucallpa?")

"Un dia y medio." ("A day and a half.")

A day and a half until I could expect any medical assistance! At that point I didn't think I'd last another full day. My priority then shifted from medical support to finding a way of getting a message back home to say that I had been shot and that I was a day and a half upriver from Pucallpa. Dying without letting anyone know where or how seemed like a very selfish way to leave those I loved behind. I envisioned that if I did not make it out of the jungle alive, my mom would forever be sitting at home waiting and hoping for me to walk magically through the door one day. I was intent on finding some form of communication, thinking that even if I did die, at least there would be some closure for my mom and those at home.

"Hay un telefono?" ("Is there a phone?") I gestured holding a hand signalled phone to my ear.

To my amazement a few people pointed to a small hut nearby. I felt a renewed surge of energy and decided to stand up and walk there. I summoned the energy to get up, but was quickly subdued by a man behind me. I turned around to see why the man had kept me sitting and as I turned around he pointed to two other villagers, who were carrying what seemed to be someone's bed. They urged me to lie on the bed as a makeshift stretcher. I moved over and lay down. Four men then hoisted me into the air and walked me towards the hut containing the telephone.

The hut was too small for the stretcher to fit inside. I attempted to get up and approach the phone myself but was again subdued. The benevolent villagers didn't want me to move at all and they pointed to a man who would dial the number for me and then hand me the phone.

"Numero?" ("Number?")

I thought for a few seconds about the number to dial. I knew my mother's number, but had to think about the dialling code.

"Ah, sero, sero. Ah, ah... Eight, ocho, um, ah, two, dos, uh, ah..."

I could not translate the numbers from English to Spanish without forgetting what I was saying. It was too difficult a task and I felt completely incapable of thinking clearly. I had the number in my head, and knew the Spanish translation for each number, but consistently forgot what I was saying as I translated it. I again internalised that I must definitely be suffering from a major brain haemorrhage.

I rolled over on the stretcher and wrote the numbers in the sand as a way to remember the digits I had already verbalised. After several slow minutes I successfully managed to translate the number. The phone had a long cord attached to the call box and the man handed me the receiver. The operator said in Spanish that the number was invalid. I attempted to call several times, adjusting the dialling code each time, but without succeeding in connecting through. All of my thinking and the effort of calling produced no result, leaving me exhausted and frustrated.

I was hoisted back to the shelter in which I had originally been sitting. Someone brought and covered me with a blanket. I was also wrapped in a plastic sheet. Most of the inquisitive people slowly moved away, as they started getting back to their usual evening routines. I was beginning to feel lethargic, so called for some more sugar water. I estimated that it had been almost three hours since I was shot and the failure to contact home on top of the debilitating situation left me completely drained. All I wanted to do was to close my eyes and fall asleep.

The sun had just set and the dark pinky-orange sky was fading into night. I didn't know what to do but started to work through all possible solutions. I thought of spending the night with the community, then finding a boat that could take me to Pucallpa the next day. The more I dwelled on that idea, the more I thought I may not be able to make what would amount to a two-day wait and journey to reach a hospital. Time was of the essence and I knew I had to get moving towards proper help as soon as possible.

"Vamos a Pucallpa!" ("We go to Pucallpa!") I yelled.

One of the men walked over to discuss the plan and despite the language difficulties, I somehow managed to communicate with him. He informed me that this community didn't have enough petrol to get me all the way to Pucallpa, so instead, they would take me downriver to the next community, which was bigger than this one and had its own doctor. I didn't know if the next village would be any better, but took comfort in the fact that they were going to help me. The man then walked off and left me lying alone on the stretcher.

Darkness had set in and several men came back to where I lay, still on the stretcher. Without words or warning, they hoisted me up and began walking me back into the jungle. The stretcher ride was bumpy as they trampled through the jungle, following the narrow path. They walked me back to the river's edge and transferred me, stretcher and all, into a small, motorised peke-peke.

They lay me in the boat with my head facing the engine and my feet at the bow. The boat was stern-heavy and the angle at which I was lying made me feel that blood was filling my throat and causing a choking sensation. I sat up and turned around so that the blood could flow downwards, thereby also opening up my air passages. I had deduced that I had severe internal bleeding and tried to determine whether the blood was filling my stomach or lungs, or both. If my lungs were being filled, I wondered how much blood it would take before I could possibly drown.

I remembered the importance of the sugar water and urged the men carrying me to bring some onto the boat. Fortunately they did, and I asked for another cup. One of the men scooped half a cup of river water and dug into a bag of sugar to mix a handful into the water. The sugar water was working wonders. I felt a surge of energy at every sip and the sweet taste overpowered the bitterness of blood.

We took off into the night, heading downriver. Four men, two behind and two in front, accompanied me on the small boat. The roar of the engine and the lapping of the water against the boat's hull drowned out the sounds of the jungle. We had no lights but there was enough moonlight to illuminate our way down the river. One of the men sat over me, placed his hand gently on my chest and began singing very softly. I peered upwards to see who he was, but the moonlight had cast a shadow over his face and all I could make out was his silhouette. He seemed to be chanting a soft rhythmic prayer that was soothing and relaxing. It reassured me that I was in caring and compassionate hands.

After what felt like just over an hour of boating, we reached the second village. We pulled up and tied the boat to several others that were all stacked like pencils in a pencil box. The men who were escorting me headed off to talk to the members of this new community, leaving me alone in the boat. I remained still, hoping that I would receive some form of medical attention soon.

20

Make or Break

I had been lying on the makeshift stretcher, in the dark, wrapped up in blankets and plastic on the stationary boat, for over an hour. The apparent lack of urgency was beginning to concern me. I had received no medical attention and as of yet there didn't seem to be any plan to get me to a hospital. Time was dragging as I waited for some assistance or initiative for the next steps to be taken.

Periodically someone would come to check on me, bringing sugar water or updating me on the current situation. However, the updates primarily revolved around the need for money in order to proceed. The people who had brought me here were discussing how to get me to the nearest hospital in Pucallpa, which was still over a day's travel away by motorboat. Each passing moment without purposeful action added to my frustration as I internalised whether they understood the severity of the situation or realised that time was of the essence? 'What could take so much time to discuss? Either we go to the hospital or we don't.'

In my concern and frustration I would shout out in my broken Spanish, "Sólo tengo unas pocas horas de vida – nosotros vamos rapidos!" In my head, this translated to, "I only have a few hours to live – we go quickly!"

It was the only way I had of encouraging some form of urgency and of expressing the need to get moving with some focussed intention. As I said this, the conversation would go quiet. The villagers would repeat what I had said and then continue their riverbank discussion, all huddled around the light of a burning lamp. Whether they understood me or not, I knew that they could hear what I was saying.

I would also shout out, "Cual es el problemo?" ("What is the problem?")

One of the locals then came over to explain the situation. From the first time that I had asked what the problem was, I had always received the same answer, "Pobre" ("Poor"). The issue seemed to be money. It bothered me that as I lay in a state of uncertainty, not knowing whether I would be alive much longer, the primary concern was money. I realised that they were a poor community who possibly didn't have the money for fuel to get me to hospital. I understood their predicament, but explained that everything I had was left behind when I was shot, even dramatically throwing off my blankets to show that all I had on was a pair of cycling shorts. My only form of surety was that I could sort out some form of payment for them once we reached Pucallpa. It seemed as if they didn't believe me and perhaps suspected that I was hiding a secret wad of money somewhere.

It felt like I had become suspended in time and no matter what I said, the locals had formulated their own idea of who I was and what I had to offer. After a further hour of discussion, all that had emerged was that they were poor and that I had no money. Again, it irked me that my welfare did not seem to be the top priority. I knew that any solution rested in the hands of the authoritative bodies of this second community – it was up to them as to whether I could expect any form of help in reaching Pucallpa. My fate lay in their hands.

I understood that petrol was an issue, but became even more frustrated when I witnessed another boat pull up alongside the one I was on, and then proceed to take off 30 minutes later. I pointed out that the boat had petrol, and that we could have used it, but they responded that the boat and driver were going the other way! I started to realise that petrol wasn't the issue, they had petrol, but instead, some of the community members saw my predicament as an opportunity for some form of reward or compensation. I also considered that perhaps they had not fully comprehended the extent of my injuries and the seriousness of the situation, and that they had figured that they had time on their side.

It had been nearly six hours since I had been shot and I began to feel where some of the shots were dispersed around my body. My muscles had started to cramp and throb around the bullet holes. The pain was intensifying. Due to the pain, I only felt comfortable lying on my right side, awkwardly balancing my body weight on my shoulder blade. I couldn't sit up or lie down completely on my back. I also felt my insides filling up from the internal bleeding. Initially I thought that the internal bleeding was draining into my lungs and I wondered again how much blood it would take before I would drown in my own blood, or before I would die from a loss of blood. Either way, I knew that my injuries were severe and that I needed a plan of action as soon as possible. I called for more sugar water.

One of the technological comforts I had brought with me on the adventure was my Kindle for reading during the nights of camping. I had been reading about tests and theories based on the placebo effect in medicine, and how sugar solutions have had positive results in all spheres of the medical field. The success was more as a result of a belief in the solution's healing properties than the effects of the solution itself. Keeping that in mind, I chose to form a belief that the sugar water I was ingesting was both a painkiller and a stimulant to keep me awake. I feared that if I fell asleep I may not wake up again.

Every time I felt drowsy, or whenever the pain intensified, I would call for sugar water. Someone would have to come over to pour a few gulps of the heavily sweetened solution into my mouth, as I was too weak to sit up and drink for myself. This would provide me with a boost of energy and a temporary relief from the pain, and the sweetness was an added bonus, as I hadn't eaten since breakfast and the taste served to satisfy my appetite.

I suspected that if the people in this new community could see the severity of my injuries, they might develop some sense of urgency. All they knew was that I had been shot, I was a foreigner and I required medical assistance. The first community had seen me in the daylight, covered in blood and mud, and just the sight of me aroused urgency. However, since we had reached the second community at night, all they had really seen was a small part of my face that was visible from my cocoon of blankets and plastic.

I had realised that the internal bleeding was a huge concern. My breathing became increasingly constrained as I literally felt my insides filling up. As my breathing became slower and shallower, it felt as if my lungs were only working at half their capacity, which was like a gradual, gargling suffocation.

Then, without warning, I began to throw up uncontrollably. In the moonlight, I could see the dark substance coming out of my mouth in projectile vomiting. I threw up all over the boat and blankets. As my vomit pooled in the boat, I noticed one man using a cup to scoop the expelled blood overboard. I was shocked by the amount of blood

I was discharging and became concerned that I may eventually pass out from a loss of blood. Seeing the blood being bailed out of the boat put into perspective just how much I had lost, and after the fourth cup, I decided to focus instead on breathing between the vomiting spells. In my body's attempt to decrease the amount of blood accumulating within, it seemed to escalate the convulsions, causing my muscles to tense, which resulted in waves of excruciating pain pulsing throughout my body. With every squeeze of my abdomen, I could feel where each shot was lodged.

To add to the discomfort, some of blood in my stomach had been there for so long that it had coagulated into a hardened, jelly-like substance. As it was being forced out through my mouth, it was choking me, so I had to push my fingers into my throat, break the clots apart and pull them out to prevent choking. This caused tremendous pain for my punctured throat. As my stomach emptied, the vomiting spell eventually ended, and I lay on the stretcher whimpering and groaning. The discomfort, blood loss and gore reminded me how intensely serious the situation was. I needed medical assistance urgently and I worried that I may not survive for another hour, let alone another day.

This gruesome scene seemed to finally capture the locals' attention. When I began vomiting they had surrounded me, watching me throughout the process. I could hear their gasps and remember one person rubbing my back as I lay there whimpering from the pain. It was a comforting rub, like the one used to burp a baby. Whoever that person was, he or she remained by my side and continued to rub my back throughout the rest of the discussion.

Fortunately, this community had access to basic medical supplies and amidst the discussions, after my vomiting, the community 'doctor' and his assistant took the initiative to attach a drip to my left arm. I was so drained of energy that I just let them take my arm and find a vein to attach the drip. If I had been livelier I would have resisted the unsanitary conditions for inserting a needle into any part of my body. I was fully conscious but allowed my body to remain limp. I suspected that the drip had been a donation from a medical organisation, as both the doctor and assistant seemed largely uninformed as to how to set it up properly. The doctor used my situation to provide a quick demonstration to his reluctant assistant. He held out my limp arm, slapped it to find a vein, wiped the area with a cloth and mock-inserted the needle. He then handed my arm to his newly appointed nurse, talking her through the process. There was barely any light and I don't know if she actually found a vein, but they seemed satisfied with their success. As soon as the needle and bag were attached, I was handed the bag and told to hold onto it. I didn't feel like I was in a position to focus on keeping a bag attached to my arm, and doubted its effectiveness given the extent of my injuries, but I did take comfort from the fact that some action was finally being taken.

As I lay waiting for a verdict on the course of action, I began to re-assess my injuries and as I did, I found some solace in my deductions. Firstly, the internal bleeding was filling up my stomach and not my lungs, so I realised I would not drown in blood. Secondly, after seeing that amount of blood loss and enduring such a distressing process, I had a new measurement of what I could endure. I was still breathing and was still alive. I had looked after my body and it was looking after me. Thirdly, it seemed that plans were beginning to take shape towards some form of action on the part of the locals. Finally, the sugar water disguised the bitter taste of the blood, and despite the vomiting it would leave a sweet taste in my mouth. Each positive was in itself a form of motivation for me to remain optimistic and hopeful.

After almost three hours of discussion, I was transferred onto another boat and we finally started moving again. I had remained conscious throughout and despite lying in one position I had managed to keep my bearings. I knew that downriver was the direction in which we needed to be heading. As we took off, I noticed that we were heading upriver. 'Why were they wasting precious fuel taking me upriver, especially after the nearly three-hour discussion about the lack of money and fuel? Had they decided that I was not worth the effort and this was their way of getting rid of me?' For a brief moment

I cynically envisioned the men tipping me overboard into the depths of the river.

I was accompanied by four individuals and soon discovered that we were heading upriver so that I could be transferred to another boat with another crew. I had forgotten that we were on a tributary adjacent to the main river. I was taken upriver, transferred and returned to where the discussions happened, and we then carried on downriver and back onto the main river, flowing towards Pucallpa and a hospital. I wasn't sure what the plan was or how they had gotten around not having the resources to get me to hospital, but I was happy that we were moving. There was finally progress in the right direction.

21

Through the Night

I had initially hoped that the departure from the second village would mean a non-stop, direct route to our intended destination. I sensed that the locals had seen enough, had finally realised the severity of my condition, and had somehow managed to collect the petrol needed for the full journey. The departure reassured me that we were officially progressing to a hospital to ensure my safety.

There was still sufficient moonlight to illuminate the river, which made for safe boating and I suspected that the locals had enough experience in negotiating these parts of the river to easily navigate the safest route to Pucallpa. All of the personal boats I had seen along my journey were the same – a narrow tree trunk that had been sawed in half and hollowed out, known as a peke-peke and similar to a conventional pirogue. Each peke-peke was about three to four metres long and about three quarters of a metre wide – just big enough for the stretcher. The boat's dart-like shape and elongated hull allowed it to glide through the water with ease. The only major difference amongst the personal boats was their motors. Some had modern 25 horsepower hand-steered engines, while others had what seemed to be a modification of a two-stroke lawnmower engine attached to a metre-long shaft that propelled the boat, by far the weaker of the two. Having seen both types of peke-pekes while paddling, I could tell the boats' motors apart by their sound. I knew that we were now powered by the louder but slower of the two engine types.

As we made steady progress, I asked, whenever it felt appropriate, how many more hours we had until we reached Pucallpa. Like an eager child on a long car trip, I wanted to know how much further to go. However, during one hour of asking, I was given figures ranging from two hours to one day. The shorter estimations would build up hope, only to be dashed by the longer ones, which made me feel that I would never get there, so I eventually stopped asking.

Around two hours after our departure from the second village, I was given another shock as we suddenly stopped on a riverbank, with everyone proceeding to get out of the boat, except for the person steering. I couldn't figure out what was going on. Five minutes earlier, we'd been heading to Pucallpa, and now we had stopped for no apparent reason. My mind began to race, as I lay motionless on the stretcher. 'Why were we stopping? Had the engine broken down? Was this as far as they were willing to take me?'

Without warning I was hoisted out of the boat on the stretcher. At that point all I could see was a steep riverbank rising about seven metres up into the dense jungle. The rest was just water and more jungle. I asked what the problem was, but I was unable to understand the answer I was given.

Once they had hoisted me out of the boat, the locals then put me down in the mud and stood around me to catch their breath. After a few short moments I was lifted again and they began heaving me up the steep riverbank and towards the jungle. I still could not understand what was going on, and remained dumbfounded at the locals' new actions. 'We surely couldn't have reached Pucallpa already?' I wondered.

I felt relatively safe as the strong looking locals hoisted the stretcher with me on it up the steep, muddy, slippery riverbank. The makeshift stretcher had no straps – it was just a flat bed with legs. I still had the drip bag in one hand and used the other to cling onto the frame of the stretcher. The last thing I wanted was to fall off and roll down the bank into the mud and water. The tensing of my muscles as I clung on, combined with the bumpy stop-start movement of being hoisted up the riverbank, caused much discomfort and pain, but I figured that any complaints or shouts of agony might offend my transporters. I remained as quiet and as still as possible, as I was hoisted up the steep riverbank and carried about 30 metres into the jungle.

When we were safely on solid ground in the jungle, the four men lowered the stretcher into some small shrubbery, as if trying to hide me, and they proceeded to head off into the night, leaving me completely alone.

"A donde vas?" ("Where are you going?") I asked, but the men walked off without replying or even acknowledging my question.

As I felt the panic of the situation, I wanted to get up and follow them, but they quickly disappeared into the dark of the jungle and before I knew it they were gone. I felt anxiety and panic setting in. 'Why were they leaving me hidden and alone in the jungle? Was this how they were going to get rid of me?'

My mind raced, 'They have probably taken me out of reach of any possible community and are going to leave me to die in the jungle!' I internalised that I may have been seen as an unnecessary burden and responsibility for the simple life of the locals and that they were finally getting rid of me in an area where they knew I would not be of further hindrance. Negativity was again starting to consume my mind and pessimism began to pervade my thoughts.

I decided to take my focus off my current situation by mentally distracting myself. I began digging into my thoughts, and I started to pool all the information on positive thinking that I had accumulated over the years. If ever there was a time to be really positive and optimistic, it was now.

I recalled the book, 'Man's Search for Meaning' by Dr Viktor Frankl. Frankl was a psychologist who survived a long stay in a concentration camp during World War II. Based on his experiences, he developed a therapy known as Logotherapy. Frankl noticed that during his stay in the prison camps, the people who could endure the most pain, and ultimately those who survived, were those who remained positive about a future beyond their present situation of despair and those who imagined a life outside of the concentration camps. His therapy revolved around an individual finding a reason, greater purpose or meaning as a way of overcoming certain immediate obstacles or ordeals.

Utilising Frankl's theory, I began to think of and visualise life at home, a life beyond lying there alone, shot and helpless in the jungle. I began thinking of all the tasty foods at my favourite restaurants, playing football, surfing and relaxing on the couch, watching a movie with Chanel. Anything that took my mind off the current situation and that created a vision of life outside the jungle kept me positive and optimistic, as I lay there alone. I used my thoughts of home as a reminder that I still had a life worth holding on to.

I was working to find a strategy that would allow a sense of calm in the moment. I focused on positive affirmations and began eliminating the negative questions that came up. I didn't know what was going on or where the locals had disappeared to, so I stopped speculating about things that were out of my control. I forced myself to believe that these individuals were good people and that they would come back to help me. I also began to recall any song or movie scene that contained the word 'survive', and would run the line or scene over in my head repetitively.

These strategies eventually formed a routine that would distract me from any negative thoughts and would get me feeling positive and optimistic, which would ultimately cause me to relax. The strategy was based on the ultimate goal of surviving and it provided a way to allow a joy and stillness in the moment. As I calmed down, I was able to listen to, and take in, the sounds of the jungle. The main sounds were of the mosquitoes buzzing around my face and the croaking and groaning of frogs. The locals may well have been only a few metres away, but it felt as if I was completely alone, and the minutes dragged to what seemed like hours. It was the loneliest and most isolated feeling I had ever experienced, but through the mental strategies I was applying, I managed to find a deep inner contentment.

I knew that the external situation was out of my control, but realised that my positive thinking was an effective way of altering my state of mind and finding some peace, calm and serenity. My thinking eliminated negativity, worry, fear and panic. I eventually began to feel very comfortable lying there alone in the jungle. I became aware of the fact that despite not being able to control my external circumstances, I could control my inner processes.

As the moments passed, I felt my confidence growing. I started to think of what my survival could possibly do for others. I envisioned being able to share an incredible survival story in the hope of empowering others and pondered that perhaps this was the real life experience I was looking for and that I deemed necessary to inspire others. My survival could be a tool for promoting positive mental strategies, a reverence for life and an optimistic outlook on living, but I could only do this if I remained alive and if I consciously applied and took note of my thoughts throughout the process of attempting to get to safety. I had reached a place of acceptance and positivity.

My sense of serenity was eventually interrupted when I heard voices coming from the dark. The locals, along with some new people, were returning. They chatted amongst themselves and then looked at me for a few moments, as if they were showing me to the new men who were accompanying them. After the brief 'show and tell' they lifted me up again and we set off deeper into the jungle. They carried me for a while and then stopped to catch their breath. Eventually we reached another spot on the river. I suspected that I had been walked over to the riverbank of a smaller tributary lying adjacent to the main river passage. They had cut across a portion of the jungle, which bypassed another community's land, and had obviously picked up the new crew members on the way.

I was then transferred to another boat with a new crew and again we set off into the night. The relief was twofold: firstly, we were, again, en route to Pucallpa, and secondly, the sound of the engine told me that we were now being powered by the faster and more modern motor. The fact that we were making progress again provided a deep sense of comfort and renewed hope.

I greeted the new crew members and thanked them politely for their kind help. I wanted to make sure that I expressed my gratitude to these men as I realised I may never see any of them again. Whenever appropriate or possible, I would reach out and pat one of the crew on the back or squeeze an arm or leg, saying a warm, "Muchas gracias señor, muchas gracias" ("Thank you very much sir, thank you very much").

After a two-hour trip in the new boat, I was transferred again. As before, I was carried up the riverbank and left alone in the jungle. I reassured myself that they were going to come back as they had done previously. I still felt the initial panic of being left alone in the jungle, but felt more at ease this second time and managed to focus more on the sights and sounds of the jungle. The men's movement and talking would cause the jungle in the immediate vicinity to fall silent, but as soon as I was left alone for a few minutes, the jungle would liven up with the usual melody of sounds. I peered through the blankets, as the mosquitoes buzzed around and landed on the small part of my face that the blankets did not cover, but for the first time I didn't mind and gave them free rein to take some more of my blood.

Even though I had already been camping alone in the jungle for weeks in a tent, lying there open, exposed and vulnerable seemed like a truly different experience. I felt a real sense of calm. I had previously imagined being alone in the jungle to be a very scary ordeal and found that just being enclosed in a tent provided a shield between the jungle and I, yet, in this new scenario, I felt safe. Perhaps it was because I had experienced the worst-case scenario and had a new standard of what was scary and daunting and what was not. Perhaps a false sense of euphoria or the nostalgia evoked by being so vulnerable in such a foreign environment caused the relaxation and complete peace in the moment. Whatever it was, I was truly amazed at how peaceful I eventually felt, lying there completely alone in the jungle.

I hadn't initially understood what the strategy of the locals ultimately entailed for getting me to hospital. It was only later that I realised that their plan of action had involved them transferring me from boat to boat along the route. The lengthy discussions at the second village must have concluded that a single direct boat trip was not possible, and that hopping from community to community and transferring from boat to boat would be the only way to get me to a hospital in Pucallpa. I became the baton passed on in a lengthy jungle relay, as each crew would hand me over to the next as the journey was broken into smaller, more manageable passages.

I suspected that my predicament may have brought these isolated communities into contact with each other for the first time in years. The fact that they had to be respectful of each community's territory and then explain the situation to the new community was probably the greatest cause of delay in getting moving. There were probably many rules and customs for how villagers could pass through another community's territory, and they most likely required permission to do so from the authority figures in each of the rural communes.

Whenever I did have company on the boat rides, I would work on my Spanish with the crew members, explaining what had happened and why I was in the Amazon area. After a bit of talking I would have to stop because my throat would hurt from the agitation of the puncture. During the quiet times, I would concentrate on my thought patterns. I was still intermittently vomiting a lot of blood, which added to the pain. The convulsing and retching would totally distract me from everything and send me into a negative spiral. I would start to dwell on the thought that I may not make the hospital in time and that I was slowly bleeding to death. I would then have to force myself to think positively, returning my mind to a calm, affirming state. I would think about home and survival, and about how every moment I was alive meant that I still had hope. I was continually building and refining my own internal strategy of motivation, inspired by constructive thought patterns and the belief in the placebo effect of the sugar water to subdue the pain and to keep me awake through the night.

As the hours passed, I used the elapsed time as another source of confidence. If I had survived one hour, I could survive another hour. If I had survived four hours, I could survive another four. From the decision to run after being shot, to the fact that I was now completely dependent on strangers for assistance, I realised that the only thing I could do was to focus on my internal state and the quality of my thinking. I firmly believed that my thinking had a part to play in my survival, and continued to reaffirm that I had looked after my body, and that it was doing the same for me.

Despite the overwhelming odds, I was still alive. Had I chosen to give up and fall asleep, I may never have woken up again. These people who were initially strangers were helping me to get to hospital, and it would have been selfish of me to give up the will to stay alive by losing consciousness. I owed it to myself and to the people helping me to do whatever I could to remain positive, awake and alive.

22

Almost There

At around six o'clock on Sunday morning, over 14 hours since I had been shot, we reached a built-up town with roads and concrete housing. I was transferred from the boat into a tuk–tuk, which meant I had to get off the stretcher and sit upright in the tiny three-wheeled taxi. Changing positions was intensely painful. My neck had become limp and it hung loosely from my shoulders. I was still holding onto the drip bag as we drove off into the town. The jarring of the tuk-tuk on the rough roads caused the puncture in my neck to bleed profusely, and after a ten-minute ride, the right side of my neck had developed a swelling the size of a tennis ball. The external wound had coagulated, leaving the puncture to bleed directly into my neck, forming a massive haematoma.

We eventually arrived at a small clinic. It was still dark and we had to knock on the windows to wake up the local doctor. I was ushered into a small room with a bed, and the doctor undressed me to inspect and assess my wounds. He took a few photos and filled out a report, but did not touch me to further inspect the bullet wounds – his assessment was purely visual. My shirt that was tied around my neck was muddy and bloody, so instead of putting it back on, I was given a robe, which I wore over my cycling shorts. I was then escorted out of the clinic, into the tuk-tuk and back towards the river. The pain intensified from all the moving, and sitting upright in the tuk-tuk again added to the discomfort.

When I returned to the riverbank, someone came up to me to see what the problem was. Everyone else just stared at me, as the rising sunlight clearly showed my bloodied face and terrible state. The intrigued individual asked what had happened. I did not have much energy, so just gestured to show a gun shooting. He seemed to understand as he expressed his concern, handing me 20 Soles and giving me a light pat on the back. Besides the locals who had helped me thus far, he was the first stranger to voluntarily make the effort to show an interest in my state, and his caring actions brightened me up. The lack of sleep and food over the past 24 hours, combined with the fact that I had been shot, left me feeling incredibly weak, and I managed only a forced wince of a smile as the kind individual walked off.

The man who had accompanied me from the clinic had gone ahead and he called me towards a small taxi boat waiting on the riverbank. I was assisted into the boat and escorted to an upright seat at the front of the covered ten-seater commuter boat. I was introduced to another man, who would be my escort to Pucallpa. He held the doctor's written report, which was to be handed to the hospital in Pucallpa. We departed at 07:30 on the Sunday morning, and I was assured that this would be the last boat ride I would have to take to reach Pucallpa – on the fastest boat available.

By mid-morning the wind had picked up and the small, fast boat slammed into the choppy water as we sped towards Pucallpa. Each slam whipped my loose neck and I began to vomit more blood. I was so weak that I made no attempt to vomit overboard. I would just vomit next to myself, letting the leftovers dribble and drool down my chin and onto my lap where the drip bag was sitting. I was still holding onto the drip bag as if it was a teddy bear, inseparable from a loving child. When the pain from the bouncing on the water became too intense, I would reach over and squeeze my escort's hand and he would signal to the driver to slow down. I suspect my bulging haematoma, flailing neck, vomiting and constant dribbling of blood and saliva would have been a bit inappropriate for the other passengers, but I was too weak and in too much pain to care how grotesque I may have appeared.

After an excruciatingly painful four hours, I noticed massive cranes peeking over the jungle walls. The sight of the cranes indicated that we were entering the port of Pucallpa, ultimately signalling the end of my journey through the jungle to safety. For the first time I began to cry, soundlessly, with just a few tears rolling down my cheeks. I ran through everything that had happened in the previous 20 hours and smiled in amazement at what I had endured.

I had experienced an emotional roller coaster, from complete and utter hopelessness to intense motivation and the power of will. I had faced a challenge that provided a greater personal insight into the depths of my own emotional intelligence and understanding of my mind. In a 20 hour period I had been exposed to the cruelty of humanity and had also experienced the incredible care and compassion within the human spirit. Despite the gruelling journey, the port of Pucallpa left me knowing without a shadow of a doubt that I was going to be okay.

As we reached the riverbank at Pucallpa I was blown away by the city's size. It was by far the largest city I had seen on the river thus far. The massive buildings and modern infrastructure brought a huge sense of relief. I had made it! It had taken just under 20 hours of travelling through the jungle at night, passing through five separate communities on various boat trips, but I had reached my destination. Those hours had felt like an eternity and at times I'd thought that I would never reach Pucallpa, but seeing the built-up city, I was happy to have finally reached some proper civilisation.

The boat docked on the riverbank and my escort helped me out of the boat and into a tuk-tuk. Many enquiring stares followed me as we drove off into the city. After a five-minute ride we reached a hospital. It didn't seem particularly modern, but it still seemed to offer proper medical assistance and I saw it as ultimately the end of my ordeal. I had done my part and assumed I was in safe hands.

23

Money Talks

Arriving at the Pucallpa Hospital, I was escorted to one of the few hospital beds. It was an open hospital that one could stroll into by accident, without realising it was a hospital at all. I had hoped that as soon as I reached the hospital, all would be taken care of and that the doctors would begin diagnosis and treatment. I caught a glimpse of myself in one of the hospital windows and saw that I wasn't in the greatest shape. The huge bulge sticking out of my neck looked like another head that was about to burst out.

For the full length of the trip to hospital, I had never once touched or tried to see my wounds. I knew that if I had felt one of the big holes in my body from the gunshot wounds, I would probably have exaggerated the injuries and my condition. I had decided from the outset that the best way to cope would be to ignore my wounds unless I was forced to address them. Initially it felt as though my back had the worst injuries, but once I'd seen my neck, I prioritised it over my other wounds, and wanted to make sure that the doctors did the same.

The first doctor I met, and the only one whose name I remembered as it was the same as my brother's, was Dr. Richard. He was one of very few Peruvians I had met who had a Western name, but despite this, Dr. Richard could not speak a word of English, nor did he seem to understand my broken Spanish. However, I did find it appropriate that of all the possible names, his was Richard. I briefly thought about my brother and realised that he had no idea what I was going through.

The doctor removed the gown and had to help remove the tight cycling shorts, as I was far too weak to undress myself. He looked all over my body, but, as with the doctor at the previous clinic, did not once touch me to examine the wounds further. He skimmed over my wounds as if he were reading a magazine containing mostly pictures and advertising, not focusing on anything specific. I kept pointing to my neck and saying, "Este es el numero uno" ("This is number one"). Dr. Richard looked me up and down a few times and then promptly left.

A nurse came to replace the drip bag that I had been clinging onto since the second village. She replaced the needle and bag and mounted it onto a proper elevated attachment. The hospital bed was in a small room, separate from any other beds. It didn't seem to be a ward; it was more like a viewing room, reception area and informal chatting space all in one. There didn't appear to be much structure or order in the hospital. I had been wheeled into a kind of nowhere zone. I noticed that the bins were all overflowing and that medical equipment was scattered carelessly over the tables and desks. It was a second-rate hospital, but a hospital nevertheless.

I had assumed that treatment would follow Dr. Richards's assessment. I lay still, waiting for treatment of any kind to commence. Just under an hour went by, with no further progress. I seemed to have been wheeled in, attended to briefly and then forgotten. I had thrown up some blood on the floor next to the bed, and it had not been cleaned up. All that had happened was that one of the open bins was moved in front of me so that I could vomit into that instead of onto the floor.

Again, the lack of urgency was concerning me. I managed to get the attention of one of the nurses and asked what the problem was. She listened, and then disappeared without an explanation. A few minutes later the man who had escorted me to Pucallpa told me that the issue was payment. The doctors would not touch me or start any form of treatment until I had guaranteed payment. I hadn't even thought this far ahead or imagined that payment would be a problem at the hospital – I'd just assumed that reaching a hospital meant safety.

The doctors also wanted proof of identity, which was another issue, as I had left everything behind in the kayak when I fled from the attackers. They wanted to know who

I was and how I was going to pay. I had travel insurance and assumed that the doctors knew this, based on the idea that they had surely dealt with foreigners injured in their territory before.

I remembered that I had saved copies of all my documentation, including my passport and insurance policy number, to my email account. Fortunately, the hospital had an Internet connection, so I was shown to the only working computer. I printed off a copy of my passport and the full travel insurance document, handed them to the nurse, and returned to the lonely hospital bed, confident that treatment would commence shortly.

However, even though I had provided the correct documentation to the doctors and staff, they seemed to have never dealt with insurance before, let alone travel insurance for a foreigner. I suspected that in their world everything was cash only. They had attempted to call the Lima office of my travel insurance company but had a problem getting through. I realised that it being a Sunday did not help the situation. I knew that they were trying to bridge the gap between the hospital and the insurance company, with their concern being around how they would receive payment. Despite their efforts, time was passing and I wasn't receiving any treatment or getting any better. I hadn't slept or eaten in over a day and a half. The payment issue was a reminder that I still couldn't relax completely. I had to make sure everything was sorted out so I could get some proper treatment and rest.

I was becoming frustrated as I started to understand the way things worked at the hospital: money was king, regardless of one's condition, race, gender or nationality. I seemed to be the only patient in the hospital, so it definitely was not a lack of staff or a capacity issue. In this environment, money seemed to equal medical attention and safety. Some staff persisted in trying to contact my travel insurance company, but after an hour they'd had no luck and I was still lying untreated on the hospital bed, thinking about a new plan.

My priority then shifted to finding a cell phone so that I could notify someone at home about what had happened and inform them that I needed help. Earlier on, a woman had approached and asked me a few questions. She had caught wind of what had happened and was interested in how she could help. In my broken Spanish, I had managed to describe my predicament, and had also told her that I needed a phone to call home. I gave her my mother's phone number and email address and she set off, intent on helping. She was unable to speak a word of English but informed me that her brother taught English at a local school, and that he would be able to translate and would get hold of my family to tell them that I needed help. She disappeared to relay the message to her brother.

I eventually managed to get Dr. Richard's attention and asked if I could borrow his cell phone. He allowed me to keep the phone and disappeared into another room. It was coming up to midday in Peru, and the seven-hour time difference meant it was going into Sunday evening in South Africa. I knew that I had to contact my mom personally as soon as possible and inform her about the situation. I didn't want to dramatise my condition, but needed to convey the basics in a brief phone call. I sent her a text message asking her to call me on Dr. Richard's number. She called within a few minutes, in an extremely worried and concerned state.

"Davey, are you okay? What is going on?"

"Mom, I have been shot. I am in a hospital in Pucallpa. They won't help me until I can show proof of payment. I need help and I think someone is going to have to fly to Peru."

She asked how serious it was, and I reassured her that I was okay, but that I did need help.

I don't think I'll ever truly know how shocking and traumatising that call must have been for my mom. The brief chat must have shaken her to her core. To call your son in a foreign country and hear him saying that he had been shot and needed help would leave any mother feeling helpless and anxious.

I hadn't even thought as to how any solutions would come from a phone call half way across the world. I imagined people receiving a call or message from my mom saying, 'My son has been shot in the Amazon Jungle – do you have any contacts or can you help?' It must have been the most foreign, if not unbelievable phone call anyone could receive. The whole situation seemed so farfetched as many people didn't even know that I was in South America, let alone the Amazon Jungle, and finding contacts in that region must have felt like an impossibility.

I hadn't realised that while I lay alone in the hospital bed, people from all over the world were beginning to network and move mountains to ensure my well being and safety.

About an hour after the phone call with my mom, and while I was lying in the bed contemplating other possible solutions, I was met by Bettina and Álvaro. They had been to several other hospitals and clinics in Pucallpa looking for me. Unbeknown to me at the time, my mom had been frantically networking to try and get me some help, and Bettina and Álvaro finding me was the result of some amazing cross continental connections. Serendipitously, SABMiller had a plant in Pucallpa, and my uncle, Andrew, who worked for them, had requested Bettina and Álvaro, who also worked for SABMiller, to come to my aid.

"You are going to be okay David, we are here to help," Bettina calmly reassured me.

Suddenly there was concern, and action was initiated. As soon as Álvaro, with the backing of SABMiller, had guaranteed the surety of payment, I was suddenly regarded as a priority. I was immediately taken to the radiology section so that proper diagnosis could begin.

As I was being wheeled in for X-rays my stepfather, Curt Wolff, called to tell me that Andrew had found someone to help me and that everything was going to be okay. I let him know that Bettina and Álvaro had already arrived and that I was in safe hands.

As I was pushed out of radiology after a few X-rays, I met Darwin. He told me that I had spoken with his sister earlier and that he'd subsequently spoken with my mother and stepfather about my condition. I reached out and thanked Darwin as I passed, and asked him to thank his sister on my behalf.

My father, Louis du Plessis, also called. He asked what had happened and I briefed him on the situation. He was working in the United States and said that he would be flying out to Peru within a day or two. I was relieved that the ball was rolling and that I was safely on the way to treatment and recovery.

I had been in this hospital for over four hours, when I was wheeled into a private room, where Bettina was waiting. The story had reached the media and the hospital was bustling with local reporters, all interested in getting details. Bettina informed me that this media attention was the reason I had been moved to a private room. She had denied all media access and had instructed a nurse to keep people out of the room. My health was priority and I had no desire to speak to anyone. I wanted rest and quiet. Two policemen were allowed to take a statement, which Bettina translated. I waited for the next steps to be taken.

Just under an hour later, the doctors came in and briefed Bettina and Álvaro on the extent of my injuries.

They had examined the X-rays and determined that this particular hospital didn't have the facilities or equipment to operate on me. I would need air support in order to be flown to Lima for proper medical assistance. I'd waited over four hours to be told this, and it frustrated me. I thought a good visual examination would have been enough to determine that the hospital could not operate, and that this could have saved some time. The doctors' lack of urgency had cost precious hours. It was nearing nightfall and the next issue was that it was considered too dangerous for helicopters or light aircraft to fly over the Peruvian Andes at night, which was required in order to reach Lima. I would have to wait until morning before I could be airlifted to Lima.

Once it became clear that all possibilities had been saturated, to no avail, I resigned myself to the fact that I would just have to wait until morning before I could expect any proper medical treatment. I handed the phone back to Bettina, who had taken the role of answering calls and updating people back home.

After eventually calming down and thinking about all that I had already endured, I figured that I could easily wait a few more hours for a flight to Lima the following day. While I lay quietly reflecting on the day's proceedings, Álvaro returned from talking to the doctors. The doctors had explained to him that my condition was extremely serious, as the X-rays had picked up shots lying close to vital organs. The urgency of the situation meant that I had to be flown to Lima to receive medical attention as soon as possible. It was decided that the only option would be to go on a commercial flight in a larger Boeing. Commercial airliners could fly over the Peruvian Andes safely at night. I could be in Lima in just over an hour on such a flight.

While I was being prepped for an ambulance transfer to the airport, I received a call from West Hansen, an American adventurer. West and his team were due to begin their paddle of the Amazon River a few weeks later and he had received word about what had happened to me. I notified him about where I had been attacked on the river, but also shared with him that, up to that point, I had actually felt relatively safe. He thanked me and said he would pass on news about my health to my mother.

I was transferred onto a proper stretcher, strapped in, and wheeled into an awaiting ambulance, accompanied by Álvaro and an assisting doctor from the Pucallpa hospital. I was rushed to the airport and straight onto the runway. My condition, accompanied by the correct documentation, allowed for the required paperwork to be done without me being present. I was loaded onto one of TACA's commercial aeroplanes, still strapped to the stretcher. The stretcher and I were placed horizontally on top of a row of four seats, with the aircraft's seat belts strapping me in. All the strapping allowed for minimal movement during the hour-long flight.

I did manage to glance over at a family sitting across the aisle from me. Their young child stared blankly at me, remaining fixated for the entire flight. I must have looked so unusual and out of place to the young boy and the fact that I had clearly visible holes in my forehead from the shots must have intrigued him! For me, the oddest sight was watching the flight attendants come down the aisles offering snacks and beverages, while I lay there harnessed to a stretcher, waiting to reach hospital. The cabin crew seemed unsure as to whether to offer me snacks or drinks too!

An hour later we landed in Lima. Once all the regular passengers had disembarked, I was carefully taken out of the plane. Álvaro and the doctor from the Pucallpa hospital were still with me as I was met by a new medical team who assisted in transferring me straight from the aircraft into an ambulance, which was waiting on the runway. Hearing the sirens as I was whisked through the city was an experience in itself. I felt like a high-profile dignitary being transported across town and I could feel that we were driving fast, zigzagging through the traffic. It also brought home the medical seriousness of my predicament.

Augusto, another SABMiller affiliate, met us at the Anglo Americana Hospital in central Lima. I thanked Álvaro and the doctor as they disappeared down a corridor to update the medical staff on my condition. Augusto and I began chatting as I lay waiting in one of the hospital wards. He told me about a friend of his in the army who had been shot several times with a rifle. He shared that his friend was still alive and was carrying on with his life as usual. I assumed that he was sharing this story as a way to reassure me and it did give me some comfort and hope. He said that the Anglo Americana was the best hospital in Lima and that I would have some top doctors attending to me in my path to recovery. One of Augusto's friends entered the room and said he had been in contact with my mother and wanted to send a photo to reassure her that I had arrived safely at the hospital.

He whipped out his phone and asked for a smile.

He joked, "Come on David, it's not that bad, give us a thumbs up!"

I chuckled as I told Augusto how ironic it was that an alcohol company had come to my aid when I didn't drink alcohol!

Augusto teased, "Perhaps now is the time to take up drinking!"

Despite my immense gratitude to the SABMiller members for coming to my aid, I certainly had no intention of starting to drink alcohol, and laughed at Augusto's banter.

I felt safe and at ease, comfortable that it was finally time to relax and let the doctors do their work. I was confident that the appropriate treatment would start shortly and that I could allow myself to fall asleep, at long last. Augusto and I bade our farewells, and as he closed the curtains behind him, I lay calmly in the hospital bed, closed my eyes and drifted off.

24

Distress Call

By Robyn Wolff

It was a quiet and relaxing Sunday afternoon. I was sitting on the couch with my new Jack Russell puppy called Amazon, named in honour of Davey's adventure. A ringing telephone interrupted the tranquillity. It was an international number, so I immediately assumed it to be a call from Davey, but was surprised to be greeted by a man with a foreign accent.

"Hello, my name is Darwin. Your son David has had an accident in the jungle and is on the way to hospital in Pucallpa."

I froze, turning numb in total horror and disbelief. What had happened to Davey? The blood drained from my body and I went into a state of panic and desperation. I was not able to get any more information from the man due to his poor English and my non-existent Spanish. To make matters worse, he was calling from a public telephone and had no more money. He said I should send him an email, which I did. My email kept bouncing back, and I assumed that in my flustered state I had not written down the email address correctly. After frantically calling the phone number several times, I was eventually greeted by someone else, who could not understand English at all. I was becoming desperate, and was fraught with anxiety. I wanted to know what had happened to my son. In my mind I speculated that he had been bitten by a snake or some other creature, or was sick.

The phone rang again. It was Darwin, and this time he gave me a cell phone number. I called him back immediately, initiating the start of my broken communication with him, and the ordeal I was about to go through.

"Darwin, what has happened to my son? What accident? Where is he? Is someone with him? How did you get my cell phone number?"

All he could convey was a repeat of what he had said in the initial call, "David has had an accident in the jungle and is on the way to hospital in Pucallpa."

I couldn't get any detailed information from Darwin due to a combination of the language barrier and his lack of knowledge on what had actually happened to Davey. As grateful as I was for Darwin's notification, the unanswered questions left more concern than comfort, as I panicked uncontrollably.

I then called my mum and gasped out in terror that something had happened to Davey. My world was falling apart and I remember holding my head, sobbing, thinking that this was the end for me. I couldn't carry on. My darling, precious son was in trouble.

I felt helpless. I was alone at home, and did not know where to begin. I felt overwhelmed and totally inadequate. I didn't know how to help my son, when he was so far away and my resources were limited. Emotionally and physically I did not know how I was going to sort this out and help Davey.

I suddenly realised that to be of value in this situation, I had to get into a zone, detach from my emotions and do something constructive. With this realisation, I immediately went onto Facebook and put out an SOS type message on Davey's adventure page, asking for anyone who could speak or translate Spanish. Fortunately, I received a reply from Sandra, the mother of one of Davey's friends. She managed to translate an email Darwin had sent, yet it still did not provide me with much more information.

I had a list of important numbers that I kept with me in case of any emergency. A few weeks earlier, I had called Pierre who had supplied Davey with his PLB. I had wanted further information about exactly how the PLB worked and wanted to update my contact details on the PLB system, as we had elected that I would be the first person to be notified if the PLB was activated. I called

Pierre again, who told me that the PLB was only traceable if activated, and at that point it had not been activated.

My mind began to run through different scenarios. Davey had previously been through a more difficult part of the Amazon where his kayak had nearly broken. He had told me that he was going to tackle that part of the river by floating on a truck tyre tube, without a life jacket, and that he would then backtrack to get his kayak. I was beyond worried; I was fretful and filled with angst. I told him just to catch a bus or boat and exclude that part of the river, but true to Davey's nature he held himself to a very high standard, and with his honest approach to life, he did not take my advice, stating that taking a bus or boat would ruin the objective of navigating the river under human power only.

After he set off on the tyre tube, I then had no communication with Davey for a while, which created anxiety of excessive proportions. I sat alone many a time through the night waiting to hear from Davey so that he could reassure me that he was safe. I sank into despair many times during his trip.

I had known that Davey was taking on a mammoth task with this journey and that the adventure came with huge risks attached, but I also realised that adventure was his calling, and was in line with what he believed and accepted as truth, so I supported him wholeheartedly in whatever he chose. Davey embodied living an authentic life, and had a fire in his heart. It would have been selfish of me to hold him back because of my fears. I encouraged and supported him, believing in him and knowing that he had what it took to face any challenge. Despite my apprehension, I was swollen with pride, admiration and overwhelming love to see him pursue his chosen calling.

Once I had received the call from Darwin, and after the call to Pierre, I went further into my list of contacts. I managed to reach Mr Moodley, our local after-hours South African Embassy representative, who then put me in touch with Mr Brown. I received a follow up call from Mr Brown, assuring me of the embassy's support and letting me know that he had already called the South African Embassy in Peru for further assistance. Fortunately Davey had acquainted himself with the South African Embassy in Peru prior to embarking on his adventure.

Just under an hour after Darwin's first call, I had still not heard from Davey directly and assumed, based on Darwin's information, that Davey was still somewhere in the jungle and en route to a hospital. I called my ex-husband, Curt Wolff, and asked him to call his brother, Andrew, who had worked in South America for SABMiller, to help me and to find someone who could speak Spanish. I wanted a Spanish speaker to call the number I had received from Darwin from within South America as the phone connection was unclear and delayed. I was desperate to get more detailed and accurate information about Davey's accident.

25

Relief!

By Robyn Wolff

Shortly after contacting Curt, I received a text from Davey asking me to call him.

"Davey, what has happened? Where are you?"

"Mom, I've been shot."

This confirmation sent a chill up my spine. I was shocked, frozen in fear.

"Are you okay? Are you going to live?" I asked Davey in a faltering voice.

He replied that he was okay, but I sensed that he wasn't good. He needed help, possibly in the form of someone flying to Peru – he'd left everything in the jungle, and the doctors were refusing to help him until he could show a guarantee of payment.

My heart sank. I went into even deeper despair. I felt helpless, not knowing what would happen to Davey, or if he would even pull through. I was sick to the stomach with crushing feelings of desperation, wishing for everything to be different and hoping that somehow this would all vanish into oblivion. I could not talk to Davey for long, as the doctor needed his phone back. Besides, there was little else I could say in that moment of complete shock.

MJ, my partner, arrived home just after the call with Davey. I remember looking at him and crying from a place of gut-wrenching despair. 'How was I going to get through this? How would I survive? If Davey died, I was certain I would too.'

I was inconsolable and fell into the deepest sadness and desperation, feelings so foreign to me that I didn't know they even existed.

MJ reassured me that Davey was going to be okay and, most importantly, that now was not the time to give up. Davey was alive, and that was all that mattered. I had to pull myself together. I then called Curt again, followed by Davey's brother (Richie), my mum, and Davey's father (Louis), to update them. At this point all that was known by them was that Davey had been involved in some kind of accident in the jungle and was on the way to a hospital. The despair was palpable and intense, and it permeated every cell in my body. Louis was in New York and said that he would get on the next plane to Lima.

MJ was my rock at this point and his ability to connect easily with people and get things done efficiently was exactly what we needed. MJ contacted Sandy Govender, Davey's travel agent. Despite the fact that it was now late on a Sunday evening, Sandy informed us that the travel insurance company had assured her that all costs would be covered. She had also organised for me to fly out to Peru within the week to join Davey. I then received news from Andrew's wife, Colleen. She informed me that they had contacts in Pucallpa and that someone from the SABMiller division in Pucallpa would go straight to the local hospital to find Davey.

Things were starting to fall into place. I called Davey back and notified him that Louis was catching the next flight from New York to Lima and that someone from SABMiller was on their way to him in hospital. The insurance company knew that he required medical assistance, and was on standby. I was also able to tell him that I would be in Peru within the week.

Telling Davey this news made me feel worthwhile as a mother. I wanted Davey to know that everything was going to be all right and that I had everything under control. I reassured him that I would take care of everything, and wanted him not to worry. I think Davey knew that between MJ and I, we would make a plan. I started to believe that I could do this and as the moments passed, I grew in confidence. Despite my traumatised state, whenever I spoke with Davey, I tried to remain as calm as possible so as not to introduce more stress into his situation.

A few short moments later, I started to receive updates from Bettina who had eventually found Davey in the hospital in Pucallpa. Her calmness reassured me that Davey was in capable hands. She updated me on his condition and what he had been through. I sensed that he had already endured the worst, and now that all the pieces were starting to gel, I started to feel that he was going to be okay.

Between the frantic phone calls and updates, I continued to post updates on Davey's Facebook page. In a very short time his story had spread like wildfire and I was starting to receive interest from the press. Along with the media interest, good wishes and messages of love and support started to pour in from people all around the world. People wanted to help in any way they could. People who knew Davey wanted to reassure me that he was going to be okay and that he was strong enough to handle the situation. It was a temporary distraction from the emptiness I was feeling.

Just before midnight, I got a call from West Hansen. He informed me that he had just spoken with Davey and assured me that he sounded all right and was on his way to another hospital.

Over an hour later I received a photo of Davey lying in a hospital bed and giving a thumbs-up. Through his unkempt hair and bushy beard, I saw his distinctive smile. He was safe. I closed my eyes and felt so grateful to everyone who had helped to get Davey to safety. I knew that he would make it. He had got this far. I knew he had a resilient nature and that he was a strong person with the heart of a lion and a reverence for life. I felt at ease and there was a sudden shift as an inner calm permeated my heart and soul.

26

Hospitalised

I awoke in a blur of confusion. My father, Louis, was standing over me teary-eyed as I gazed at the ceiling in a daze. I had been sedated and was waking up from a much needed sleep. It was the first sleep I had enjoyed in over two days and had my dad not woken me, I probably would have slept for another day. I had a drip in each arm, with suction cups pasted all over my chest and back, and I could hear a heart rate monitor beeping rhythmically in the background, but had no idea where I was. It took a few moments for me to realise that I was in hospital. I'd somehow wished that everything I had experienced in the preceding two days had been nothing but a strange dream.

I had spoken with my father on the phone just as I was being wheeled out of the first hospital and transferred to the ambulance that took me to the airport in Pucallpa. He had heard what had happened via my mother and he updated me that he would be catching the next flight out of New York to meet me in Lima. Now he was standing by my side.

I could see that my dad was emotional and understandably shaken. I suspect that he hadn't known whether he would be seeing or hearing from me again after our previous phone call. His eyes welled up with tears but he held them back and expressed his joy that I was okay. He told me that this had been a big shock for everyone. He shared his military experience and noted that if I had been shot with a rifle or any other heavy artillery I would probably not be alive – I was very lucky that it was a shotgun. It then made sense how I felt so many isolated wounds peppered around my body.

I attempted to sit up but was quickly subdued by the nurses. They insisted that I lie flat on the bed. I wanted to tell my father everything that had happened in the jungle but was quickly sidetracked by hunger. I wanted to eat. I asked for some food, as I hadn't eaten since Saturday's breakfast and it was now Monday afternoon. I was refused food, however, as I was on standby for surgery.

While I was sedated, the doctors had taken X-rays of my face, neck, chest and abdomen. From the X-rays they had discovered that I had a pellet lodged in my heart. This was considered the main priority and they were monitoring it to see what it would do. If it moved, I would require surgery. I was too hungry to ask for more details about my injuries and just wanted something to relieve my hunger.

While I was asleep, the doctors had told my father that the pellet in my heart had passed through my lung and the wall of my heart, landing perfectly positioned in the septum of the heart. Retrieving the pellet would require open-heart surgery – a procedure that would possibly involve removing my heart from my chest cavity and operating on it separately. That would be a huge surgical procedure and because I had already been living with the lodged pellet for almost two days, they opted to rather leave it where it was, while monitoring it with every scan possible. If it didn't move, they would leave it; if it moved, they would have no choice but to operate. The doctors had no specific plan, and didn't know exactly how my heart would react to the pellet. I would be on standby for the next couple of days, which meant no food. It dawned on me that I might not be able to eat for the next week!

I decided to distract myself from the hunger by sharing the story of what had happened, with my dad, and elaborated further on my experiences in the jungle. I had great difficulty speaking. My breathing was laboured and I would have to take gulps of air, and speak in short phrases, not full sentences. My speech was heavy and slow and it felt very weird to be taking so long to say what I wanted to say.

My dad knew just how lucky I was to be alive. I would be continually monitored as the doctors assessed my condition and injuries. The next couple of days in hospital would involve numerous scans, tests and X-rays. I anxiously hoped that all the results would show that I didn't need surgery and that I didn't have any other severe injuries.

Visiting hours were an hour in the afternoon and an hour before lunch. My father was staying in a hotel a block away from the hospital. He would be in Lima for the next five days, and then my mom would take over. No one knew how long my hospital stay would be, but I was relieved that I would at least have family support on my path to recovery. At the end of visiting hours, my dad would go back to his hotel, assuring me that he would be back the following morning with more updates from home. I tried my luck once more and asked the nurses for some food, but they declined and I drifted back to sleep.

That evening, I was woken abruptly by two doctors wanting to do a chest and abdomen sonogram. They said there was bloating in my chest and that the X-rays had illustrated that my lungs were full of blood. They quickly ascertained that the internal bleeding, caused by the piercing shots, had formed a pneumothorax due to the presence of air and blood in my pleural cavity, which was causing the bloating. One of my lungs had been punctured and some of the internal bleeding had leaked into my thoracic cavity. This had to be drained, so they needed to operate. The operation involved puncturing the skin between my ribs and forcing a tube into my thoracic cavity. This tube would be attached to a briefcase-sized container. The imbalance of pressure would cause the blood in the thorax to drain into the case. I looked at the case, then at the size of the tube, and pleaded with the doctors to sedate me, as I couldn't bear the thought of being awake while they forced a hosepipe-sized tube between my ribs. The doctors insisted that I didn't need to be put to sleep, and that a local anaesthetic would suffice.

Within a few minutes I was prepped, with the local anaesthetic administered and a small team of two nurses and a doctor ready to operate. As soon as the appropriate area in my body was numb, I closed my eyes tightly. I felt queasy knowing that I was being sliced open and having my ribcage tampered with while I was awake. Although I was numb to all pain, I could feel the pressure and pulling as the doctor inserted the pipe. I remember opening my eyes and catching a glimpse of one of the nurse's faces. Even though part of her face was covered by her mask, I could see her wincing, with her facial muscles straining as she forced my ribs apart. I quickly looked away, vowing to keep my eyes closed for the rest of the procedure!

Half an hour later, the doctor was finished. I lay with a giant tube hanging out of the left side of my ribcage. A nurse administered some morphine, and I slowly drifted off into another deep sleep.

27

Hunger Relief

I awoke the next morning to the sounds of the ICU ward shift change. I noticed breakfast trolleys being wheeled in and I was immediately reminded of my hunger. I pleaded for something to eat, even just a piece of toast or a few slices of an apple. I was going into my fourth day of no food, but since I was still on standby for surgery, it meant no eating. I was beginning to feel very sick. All the medicine on an empty stomach was giving me headaches and causing nausea, yet I was continuously being fed pills, along with the medicine being administered intravenously. I tried to refuse my morning medicine until I could have some food. The nurse insisted that I take the pills and wouldn't leave my bedside until I did so.

My father arrived, and I pointed to the new tube I'd been fitted with during the night. The accompanying case was now ¾ full of my blood. I was amazed at how much blood there had been within my thorax. My father had known that I was going to have the chest tube fitted, but had decided not to tell me, thinking it better that it come from the doctors.

Our conversation then turned to guests. There were a few people outside who wished to visit, including some reporters. The only person I knew in Peru was my dad, so why did I have visitors? My story had apparently become topical, and was making headlines in the South African media. The incident had captivated the public. My family were inundated with media requests, as everyone wanted to know about 'the guy who'd been shot in the Amazon'. In ICU I had no access to the outside world, aside from my father's updates. The more I learnt about the interest in my story, the more overwhelmed I began to feel. I told my father I didn't want anyone in the ward but him. I was not in a position to start speaking to strangers about what had happened in the jungle, nor was I prepared to relive the experience. Not just yet.

I returned my focus back to food. I asked my dad to reason with the doctors to allow me something to eat. If the doctors said yes, the nurses would have to listen to them and feed me. Fortunately, the doctors agreed to let me have some food and an hour later I saw a trolley being wheeled in my direction. Food at last!

The plate was covered with a bowl, like a teasing surprise. I lifted the bowl and to my disappointment saw that it covered a smaller bowl containing nothing but two peas and a carrot in hot water! I was shocked. After four days of no food, was this all I would receive? The dietician knew that I was a vegan, meaning that I ate no animal products (no meat, cheese, eggs or dairy), but never did I expect this. Was it a joke? Where was the rest of my food? The nurses said this was all I was allowed. This was dismal and I was not impressed. I realised that I was going to have to make my own plan for food and asked my father if he would please go to the nearest store, get me some fresh fruit and sneak it into the ward.

On top of the miniscule meal they presented to me, the nurses wanted to administer medicine along with the pea and carrot water. I flatly refused. The medicine was making me feel sicker by the day. While I realised that the nurses had a job to do, my body could no longer handle the copious amounts of medicine without adequate food.

A few moments later, my dad returned with two bananas, an apple and an orange. I pulled them out in front of one of the nurses and began eating them defiantly. The nurse tried to interfere, but I had finished all but the orange before she had the time to take my fruit away!

Within minutes I felt stronger and healthier. The fruit had boosted my morale and the hunger had faded. I put a big smile on my face and showed the nurse the banana peel, pointing and showing her that this was my medicine. She remained unimpressed.

As part of the doctors' ongoing assessments, I was continually wheeled in and out of ICU for more scans and X-rays. In addition to the daily face, neck and chest X-rays, I was given multiple sonograms to monitor the pneumothorax. The case attached to the tube filled once, and its replacement levelled off at just over ¼ in volume. I was taken for a venogram, where a dye was mixed into the blood to track how my blood moved through the circulatory system. The venogram quickly picked up a punctured carotid artery in my neck. A pellet had almost completely severed the artery, which had formed an aneurysm. This was what had initially caused the haematoma in my neck. One of the positives of the long journey through the jungle to the hospital was that I had lived for over a day with my injuries before receiving medical treatment, so my body was already in the process of healing itself.

I had multiple MRI scans to ascertain the position of the pellets in my body and to track their movement, with the one in my heart being monitored the most closely. We counted 22 pellets dispersed all over my neck, back and head, and I was given a CAT scan to see what damage the pellets in my head may have caused. Fortunately, my skull had prevented the pellets from accessing my brain. The pellets, made of a soft lead, flattened on impact and remained squashed and embedded in my skull. My initial belief and self-diagnosis, at the first jungle community, that I was experiencing a brain haemorrhage, was due to one of the pellets damaging a facial nerve, which resulted in the loss of feeling on the right side of my face. Another pellet had gone through the ear and had lodged itself in the ear canal, which had resulted in a temporary loss of hearing.

I was left mesmerised by all the X-rays and scans and was in awe of the body and its ability to survive. I felt humbled to see that all of the body's complex functions were geared towards one priority – to sustain life. All the scans and pictures gave me an intricate view of how the body worked. The chance to view my own body from the inside made me relieved and proud that I had taken care of myself and nurtured my health. I had been eating wholesomely, was reaffirmed in my choice of diet and was amazed at the abilities of a body that worked well. Seeing the inner workings of the body further emphasised the importance of always looking after myself. It reminded me of the importance of paying a deep respect to this amazing physical vehicle of life.

28

The Road to Recovery

My mom arrived on the Friday morning, six days after I had been shot, and just before I was to go for my first major surgery. She burst into tears at the sight of me and I suspect it must have been a result of a combination of seeing her son in a hospital bed attached to machines, and the greatest relief to finally see with her own eyes that I was alive. My father had been keeping her updated on my progress. Even though I considered myself to be an independent young man and resilient adventurer, it was reassuring to have my mother by my side. I felt safe and comforted.

My heart seemed to be functioning normally, so the doctors decided to shift their priority to my punctured carotid artery. I was booked for surgery in which the doctors would use an endoscope to view the punctured artery. The procedure required puncturing my groin and sending a tiny camera all the way up into my neck through the artery. They would assess the damage to the artery from the inside using the camera. At the same time, they would remove as many surface pellets, those lodged no further than an inch from the surface of my skin, as possible. My body was already in the process of healing, and retrieving pellets lodged any deeper than this could cause further damage rather than relief. The tube in my chest would also be removed during the surgery.

Through the surgery, the doctors discovered that the issue with the punctured artery was the position of the wound, which made it difficult for them to reach. To mend the punctured artery, the doctors would normally cut open the neck and stitch the severed wall of the artery, but due to the position of this puncture, the only way to access it was through the jaw, and this would have involved cutting my jawbone in half. Such massive surgery was considered invasive and unnecessary. The next best option was to get a custom-fitted stent that could be pushed up into the neck via the groin and that would form an artificial arterial wall on which the artery could mend itself from the inside.

I was still receiving multiple visitation requests but refused the majority. I knew that people were concerned, but I simply didn't have the energy or desire to engage with strangers. I had been journeying alone for the prior two months and was adjusting to life in the hospital. I was used to being in solitude and still enjoyed my time alone

The Peruvian Andes

The Abra Malaga pass

Cycling through the jungle

Tubing the Amazon

Walking along the river bank

My foldable kayak

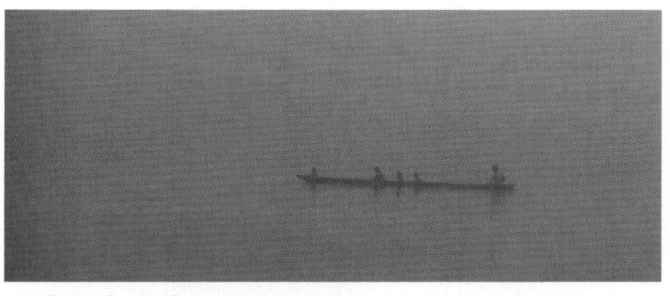

A peke-peke in the morning mist

A developing storm

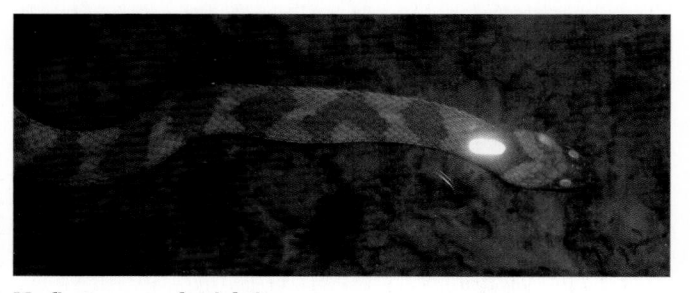

My first anaconda sighting

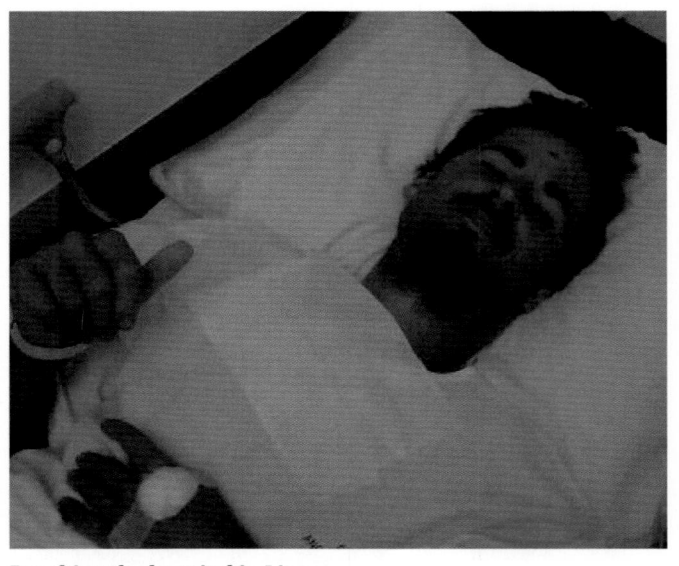

Reaching the hospital in Lima

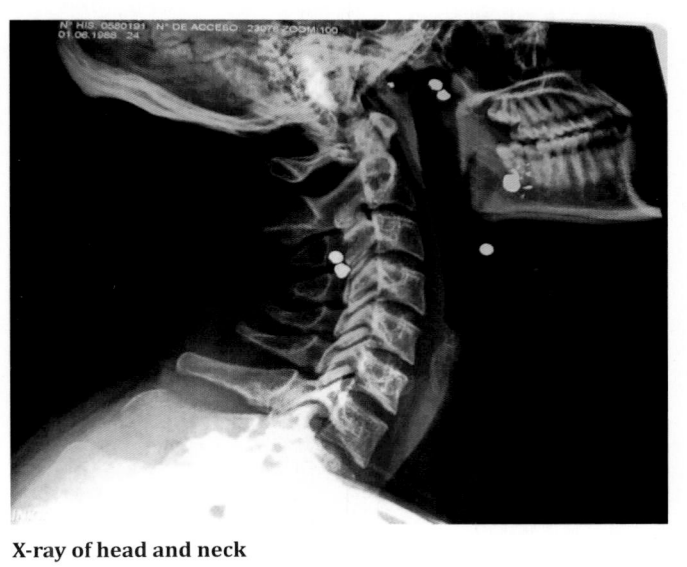

X-ray of head and neck

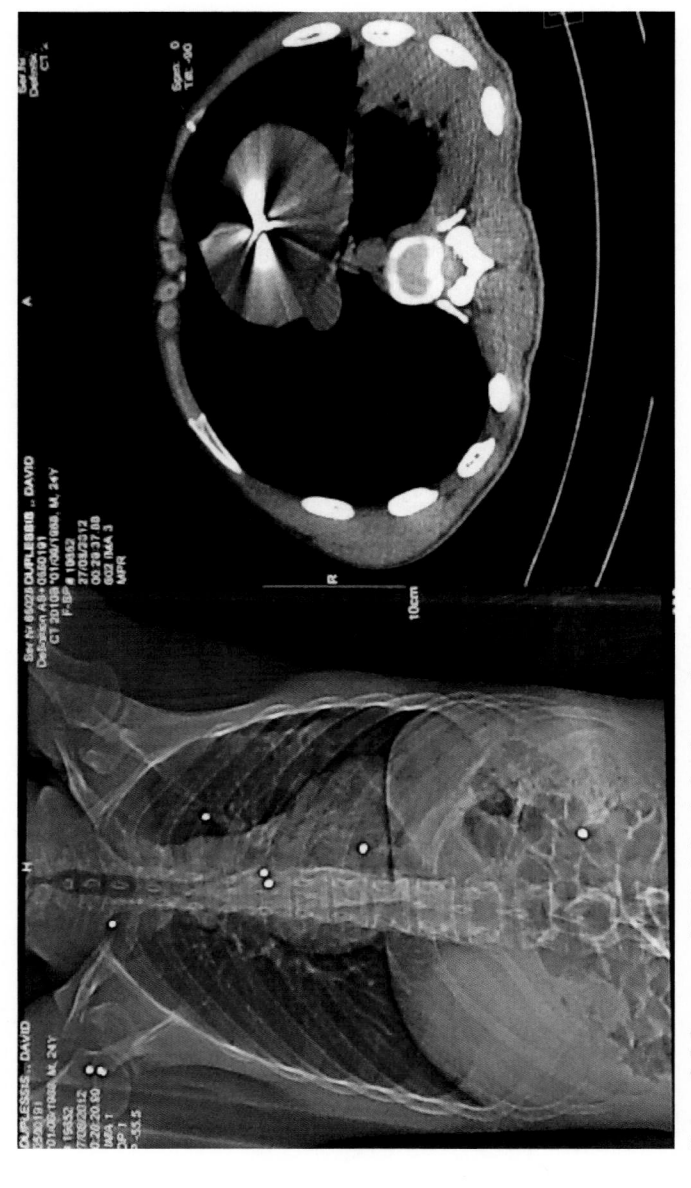

X-ray of abdomen and MRI of shot lodged in my heart

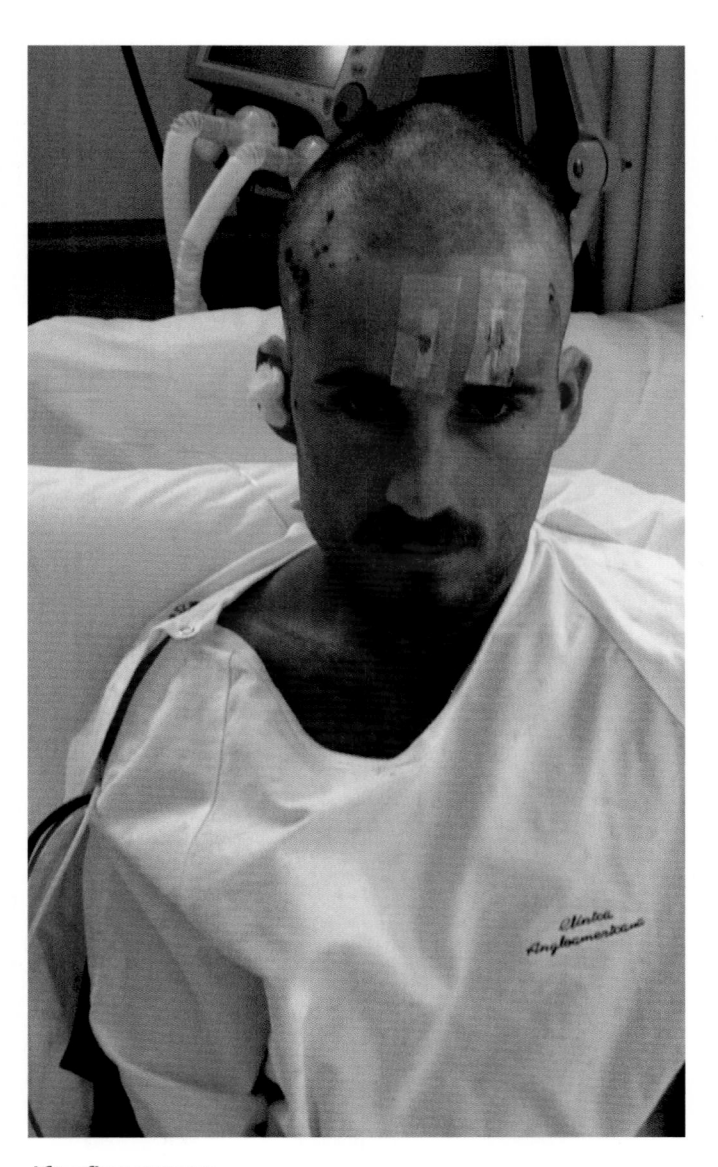

After first surgery

sitting in the ward. I used my time to put pen to paper as my way of fully comprehending what I had been through.

As I internalised and reflected on my ordeal, I initially began to feel somewhat disappointed. I had failed in my attempt to navigate the Amazon from source to sea. Even though the events that ended the adventure were beyond my control, I still felt as if I had failed in what I had set out to do.

I had put over a year's preparation into reaching the Brazilian coastline. I had endured every difficulty that I was challenged with by constantly anticipating my eventual arrival at the Atlantic coast and the taste of the salt water in my mouth. I had maintained motivation and stayed focused by aiming to achieve the eventual goal of being one of the very few who have had the opportunity to journey the Amazon River from its source to its meeting with the sea. I had been making good progress, was prepared for the dangers I had anticipated and had been adjusting to my new environment. My dreams were banished within a few moments. I was disappointed and frustrated by how my aspirations had been pulled out from under me within a few seconds. I would be in hospital for nearly a month, and knew that attempting to go back onto the river after that would be irresponsible and selfish. The adventure was over.

In one of our conversations, my dad told me that my stepbrother William had decided that he was going to change his name. I recalled, when I was younger, telling my dad that I too wanted to change my surname, from 'du Plessis' to 'Spence', my mother's maiden name. When I was a child, it had bothered me that many of my peers could not pronounce my surname correctly, nor could they understand why it didn't start with a capital letter. It is properly pronounced 'doo Ple-sea', but most pronounced it 'du Ple-siss'. As I grew older, I had learnt to appreciate my surname, but I could still understand William's desire for the name change. I could sense that my dad felt the same disappointment he expressed when I had wanted to change my name, as he came from a family with a proud heritage. The 'du Plessis' name ran in his blood and it was a strong surname that reminded him of his identity. I asked my dad what William wanted to change his name to, suspecting that he too wanted to take his mother's maiden name.

"David, William wants to change his name to Brad!"

For the first time in weeks, I laughed. I laughed until tears came out, and then had to subdue myself because moving my chest was incredibly painful. We both chuckled at the irony of William wanting to change his forename and not his surname. It was good to be able to laugh again. All my disappointment seemed to disappear in that good laugh. It seems that perhaps sometimes laughter is the best medicine after all. I was starting to come to terms with the fact that the Amazon project was prematurely over. I was also starting to appreciate that I was alive and felt an immense gratitude to all those who had helped me.

When it came time for my father to go back to the United States, I was glad that my mother was there for emotional support. I told her everything about the shooting, but as I started to elaborate, she told me she didn't want to hear the details. She was just happy that I was alive and that we were focused on my recovery. Before he departed, my father had updated my mom about my condition and what the projections were for my recovery: I still had a good two weeks of hospital time to expect. During the first operation, the doctors had successfully removed eight pellets, located the puncture in my carotid artery and confirmed the need for a stent, which they would emplace as soon as it arrived from Memphis, USA. They left most of the pellets in my body and would monitor them, assuming that my body would naturally coat them with tissue and either slowly push them to the surface or keep them in the same place. The pellet in my heart was still being monitored closely, and surgery would only be considered as a last resort.

I had been in ICU for over ten days. I was starting to stabilise and the nurses slowly began introducing rehabilitation exercises for me to do. They assisted in getting me walking again, and made sure I was eating at least three times a day. I had lost over 17 kilograms in the short period. I looked almost rake-like, which made my condition seem worse. Even though I felt healthy, my mom was still concerned about my welfare, getting information from the medical staff at every opportunity.

The language barrier made communication difficult and my mom was often left with unanswered questions, which further added to her worried state. I could see she was putting on a brave face but her red, puffy eyes showed that she cried every day. I could only imagine the pain she had endured. She was my biggest fan and constant motivator and knew about all the difficulties I had experienced. My shooting had thrown her into the deep end.

She told me that my story had spread in South Africa and that she was being inundated with requests from radio, TV and news channel representatives, all wanting to get updates on the story. I had not given an account of events to anyone except my father so most of the news stories were hearsay. I was still receiving numerous visitation requests and as I started to feel healthier, I decided to let my mom screen the visitors before they came in. I knew that if she liked and connected with them, I probably would too. Most importantly, my mom needed someone on the outside who could help her to find her way round the city when she was not visiting me.

On day twelve of my hospital stay, I was temporarily discharged from hospital and would be an outpatient until the stent arrived. I was to take my recovery slowly, but was allowed to walk around. I had to return to the hospital every second day for a basic check-up and for sonograms of the aneurysm in my neck. After a week, I would return to have the stent emplaced and after another three or four days recovering from that procedure, I could fly back to South Africa.

I was still shockingly thin, so my outpatient days consisted of short walks and eating as much fruit and vegetables as I could manage. I was happy to be outside and to able to feel the warmth of the sun on my skin again. I got into contact with my family and Chanel, updating them all about my situation. It seemed that my experience had shaken everyone. Chanel had been calling me weekly to track my progress during the journey, but having been in a more isolated part of the jungle, I had not spoken with her for over two weeks. It was good to hear her voice again.

I had been living with my brother before I departed for the Amazon and had last spoken with him on his birthday, just over a week before I was shot. Speaking with him always brings a smile to my face. I soon realised that everyone close to me had taken a big knock. I suspect it was the not knowing what had happened that caused the greatest anxiety for them. For my relatives and loved ones it was as if I had been in a state of limbo on the trip, with them never knowing where I was or if I was alive, dead or dying. I assured everyone that I was healthy and recovering and that I would be home soon.

A week later I was re-admitted to hospital to have the stent emplaced. It would be a straightforward procedure and I was relieved that I could return home after that. Waiting for the stent to arrive had caused time to slow down and the aneurysm in my neck was worsening each day. The anxious wait weighed heavily on my mom. She was completely out of her comfort zone and felt fully responsible for my well being as an outpatient.

While I was in surgery having the stent fitted, Francoise and Gerhard, the German couple I had met a few weeks earlier in the jungle, visited the hospital. They had heard about the shooting and as they had lost a son to the jungle, showed great concern. The operation, which was meant to take two hours, took four, and by the time I was released into ICU, the couple had left. My mom told me they'd come and that they were deeply moved by my ordeal. She said they'd all cried together, sharing their accounts of the stress that adventurous children cause their parents, and realising that it was something that those adventurous children would only understand when they had children of their own.

While I was recovering from the anaesthetic, my mom had managed to talk to one of my surgeons. He was amazed by my recovery and how lucky I was to have survived the shooting – and by the good fortune of where and how the shots where positioned.

"The number of pellets and where they impacted the body could have had numerous outcomes," he'd said.

But what amazed him the most was that I had managed to run with my injuries, and that I had kept calm during the journey towards acquiring proper medical assistance. The main injuries were a punctured heart, punctured lung, punctured windpipe and punctured carotid artery, as well as severe internal bleeding. Each of these injuries would usually require immediate medical assistance and they were all closely related to physical activity and psychological stress. In any heightened activity or stressful situation, heart rate, lung function and blood flow all increase, which in my case would have worsened the impact of the injuries on my body.

The first X-rays had revealed that my lungs contained a lot of blood. Fortunately, the puncture had allowed most of the blood to drain into my thorax, preventing me from drowning, but the other lung was almost half full. The fact that I had managed to run and remain conscious and calm throughout the incident, given the extent of the injuries, amazed the team of doctors assigned to my recovery.

"Your son is very, very lucky to be alive," the surgeon remarked. My mom agreed.

The stent was successfully emplaced and three days later I was discharged. I had spent just under a month in and out of hospital. I was recovering daily and looking forward to getting home. As soon as we had received written confirmation that I was fit to fly, our return tickets were booked.

29

Reflections

Amazingly, a day before my departure, as we were making preparations to leave Peru, I received an email stating that my PLB had been activated and was transmitting an SOS and its GPS co-ordinates! The PLB company had been informed about what had happened, so were aware that I had been separated from my PLB. The men who had shot me and taken my belongings were obviously fiddling with my equipment, and must have activated the PLB. They were carrying on as usual, somewhere in the jungle. I could not believe it. I imagined the two men digging through my equipment and trying on my clothes, laughing and making jokes. I envisioned the men joking that they had shot a gringo, and that getting all of his equipment was a bonus. I doubted that they felt even the slightest remorse or if they had the faintest idea that I had survived.

I tried to piece together why they had chosen to shoot me, and started to vividly recall the ambush and attack. Between trying to figure out the men's mentality and reliving the ambush, I stopped myself with the realisation that I could not allow myself to sit and wonder why they had done what they had done. I would never understand why they had ambushed and attacked me. If I chose to, I could spend the rest of my life wondering, but to linger on those thoughts would mean I would forever remain a victim. I could choose to build up anger and hatred or choose to accept that I would never know why they shot me. What had happened had happened and I decided that I would let it be.

The activation of the PLB made the entire incident feel so real again, and I remained deep in thought. I knew that I had experienced the unpleasant side of humanity and that these two individuals could cause me to lose any hope in the compassion and kindness that I had spent so many years believing in and cultivating. Despite the heartlessness expressed by the two men, I knew I had to shift my focus to the good. I recalled the old lady washing my feet, the man who placed his hand on my chest and sat by my side singing and praying, the person who rubbed my back as I was throwing up, and those men who tirelessly transported me through the jungle.

I would not let two individuals distort my views on the people I had met in the jungle and on the compassion within humankind. Entire communities had come together and pooled whatever resources they could to assist me, an injured stranger. Communities totally shut off from the outside world had united in the interest of one outsider's welfare. I was attacked by two men, yet protected and cared for by hundreds, from those hidden in the jungle to those around the globe who had gone out of their way to assist my mom during her ordeal. Ironically, it was the cruelty that had ultimately provided the evidence that there is still much compassion and good within humankind. Perhaps I had needed to experience senseless cruelty to validate and reinforce my beliefs in the inherent good and compassion of humanity.

I realised it was my choice how to perceive the entire experience. I could be angry and lose hope, or choose acceptance and remain positive and hopeful. I had sufficient real-life evidence to justify either of the choices. I chose, in that moment, to leave all of the unanswerable questions and any desire to seek justice behind in the jungle. I would depart from Peru without anger, remorse or a need for revenge. Instead I would focus on the realisations about the power of compassion, kindness and acceptance, including reinforced beliefs towards the amazing potential of the body and mind.

I asked Chanel to meet us the airport when we arrived and my mom had asked my grandmother and aunt to be there too. Given the interest in my story, I decided it would be best to enter South Africa as quietly as possible. My medical condition permitted us to fly first class all the way home. My travel insurance had been excellent throughout the ordeal and the first-class ticket home, though a necessity, was still a much appreciated and well-received treat. I was looking forward to returning home to see my loved ones and to being on South African soil again.

As we took off from Lima's international airport, I began to recall what I had experienced: the cold, raw beauty of the Peruvian Andes, the majestic, towering trees and wide, winding rivers of the Amazon Jungle, the amazing bird life, the loud creatures that kept me awake every night, the camping alone in the jungle, and the amazing and interesting people I had encountered throughout my travels. My journey had come to a premature end, my hopes had been dashed and my goals had disappeared in an instant. I was left with a new, totally unexpected experience – something I could never have imagined, but an incredible experience nonetheless.

I had failed in my first solo adventure, an attempt to navigate the Amazon River from its source high in the Andes to its meeting with the Atlantic Ocean. Instead, I had received a taste of the wondrous life of the Amazon Jungle. I was touched by the compassion and kindness I had experienced on my path to recovery, amazed at how so many had united to ensure my safety and humbled by my will and ability to survive.

After many years of pursuing an incredible story, hoping that adventure would be the source of an inspiring tale – I had received one. It was a story of facing fear, rising above challenges, overcoming the odds and never giving up or letting negativity weigh me down. I had received the incredible story I had always wanted, the story that would give me confidence when sharing the experience on a public platform and a story that proved a congruency and authenticity in my beliefs, thoughts and actions.

I had initially been clouded in judgement and hadn't realised the full scale of the incident until I was out of hospital, up in the air and on my way home. Leaving Peru provided clarity and the realisation that my survival was not a story of my own. My ego was holding onto the desire of self-praise and self-admiration based on what I had experienced. I had a resilience and mental strategy that allowed a sense of calm and peace during the incident. I was also able to acknowledge that I had looked after my body through the years, which had given me confidence that my body could heal and look after itself in the most crucial moments, but these factors were not what ultimately ensured my survival nor were they any special character traits that only I was capable of applying.

What ultimately allowed my survival was the help and care of so many initial strangers, and the small acts of compassion and kindness that gave me hope in the crucial moments to apply my strategy to survive. It was hope that inspired the choice to live and hope in the compassion of humankind that motivated the choice to carry on even when I didn't know how things would work out. I had survived, simply by the fact that when I was knocked down, there were people to lift me back up again.

No matter how positive, motivated and optimistic I was, if I hadn't received the support that I had from the communities in the jungle, I would have eventually perished somewhere in the Amazon. I had lost the idea of an ego driven story and substituted it with a story of the unlimited potential within the integrated and collective spirit of humanity, realising that the power lies within many having the same values and driving forces and not in the mindset of one.

The brief period between journeying from Peru back to South Africa was sufficient to help me recalibrate just who I was going to be, what I was going to share and how I was to be portrayed when landing back in home territory. My spirit for adventure remained as strong as it had ever been and was further reinforced in the knowing that no matter the outcome of an adventure, I will forever remain in search of more stories to share and more adventures to attempt. I wish for my life to be a beacon of hope, a symbol for the good within humanity and a platform to inspire others to be guided by compassion and to live in service to all humankind and nature.

It was a warming feeling to set foot upon South African soil again, and seeing Chanel and my family lifted my spirits. On the short car ride home, no one asked about what had happened, as though I had never left for South America in the first place. Life started to feel normal again.

Arriving home, I noticed an immediate relief, as though a huge weight had been lifted off my mom's shoulders. We dropped our luggage at the door and I turned to my mom and uttered a simple, "Thank you, Mom." She smiled and I walked through to the garden to meet and play with the new Jack Russell puppy named Amazon!

DAVEY DU PLESSIS

Davey du Plessis is an explorer, author and public speaker, as well as a passionate, determined and charismatic human being. He is driven by his quest to make a positive difference in the world, actively encouraging self empowerment and individual responsibility, while promoting a take action approach to life.

Davey utilises adventure as a source of experience to further understand the nature of humanity, as well as an avenue for opportunities that demonstrate the unlimited potential of the human spirit. His compassion towards the environment and animal kingdom and his belief that all life should be respected and protected, reflects in his choice of a plant-based diet and lifestyle.

www.daveyduplessis.com